Take My Yoga

The Wisdom of Yoga for Christians and Seekers

Take My Yoga

The Wisdom of Yoga for Christians and Seekers

Ian John Spencer

MANTRA BOOKS

London, UK
Washington, DC, USA

CollectiveInk

First published by Mantra Books, 2026
Mantra Books is an imprint of Collective Ink Ltd.,
Unit 11, Shepperton House, 89 Shepperton Road, London, N1 3DF
office@collectiveinkbooks.com
www.collectiveinkbooks.com
www.mantra-books.net

For distributor details and how to order please visit the 'Ordering' section on our website.

ISBN: 978 1 917991 15 5
978 1 917991 16 2 (ebook)
Library of Congress Control Number: 2025941769

A CIP catalogue record for this book is available from the British Library.

Design: Lapiz Digital Services

UK: Printed and bound by CPI Group (UK) Ltd, Croydon, CR0 4YY
Printed in North America by CPI GPS partners

The manufacturer's authorised representative in the EU for product safety is:
eucomply OÜ - Pärnu mnt 139b-14, 11317 Tallinn, Estonia,
hello@eucompliancepartner.com, www.eucompliancepartner.com

This book is dedicated to my wife, who first introduced me to yoga in the 1980s, and who has travelled the interfaith journey with me ever since.

Contents

Forword

In this beautifully written and highly accessible book, Ian Spencer brings together his extensive experience as both an Anglican priest and also a yoga teacher, to show how the practice of yoga can enrich and deepen the practice of Christian discipleship. Devoid of unnecessary technical language, the relative brevity of this book should not be taken to belie its depth of wisdom. What comes across from every page is the wonderful way in which the author has clearly integrated in his own life – yoked together into one unified practice – two seemingly different traditions. As he suggests, though, the practice of yoga and the lived experience and teaching of Jesus are both orientated alike to the realisation of union – yoga. This slim volume deserves to be widely read and, above all, used. It could easily become the companion of a lifetime, inviting those who are already Christian to appreciate what the practice of yoga can give them, and those who might practise yoga as a form of exercise and yet who are looking for something more, to discover that the Christian path might be the very thing they are looking for. More than anything else, though, this book entices its readers to bring it to life through their lived experience. This is a book that could transform the lives of anyone into whose hands it falls. What a gift!

—The Revd Canon Dr Christopher Collingwood, Canon Emeritus of York Minster

Introduction

"Take My Yoga and Learn of Me"

> Come to me, all you that are weary and are carrying heavy burdens, and I will give you rest.
> Take my [yoga] upon you and learn from me, for I am gentle and humble in heart,
> And you will find rest for your souls
> For my [yoga] is easy, and my burden is light.

The original passage from the Bible (St Matthew, Chapter 11 verses 28–30) is well known and often quoted within the Christian faith, particularly as a passage to encourage those who are struggling with the complexities and burdens of life. They're words of comfort, intimate and loving, an invitation to find both rest and guidance in times of turmoil and confusion.

However, if you know the passage you'll have noticed that one of the words above is a bit different to what we're used to seeing.

The word that has changed is of course "yoke". The biblical text has the word yoke, not yoga, so how come I've taken the liberty of changing it to "yoga"?

First let me state that I have no quibble that the word Jesus actually used was Aramaic for yoke, but the word yoke and yoga are closely related, so I've no trouble transposing them for good reason, which is to help us see Jesus's call in a deeper way. If we use yoga rather than yoke, we discover a new depth to this passage, and indeed very possibly all of Jesus's teachings and actions. That's what makes this apparently small change so exciting and the reason for writing this book.

Yoke and Yoga

The word yoga and yoke both have the same root, that is, they share a common "mother-word", the word from which they both derive. That word is the Sanskrit (ancient Indo-European language) word *yuj*.

Yuj means to join, to yoke together, to unify. We can see how this works when we take the actual example of what a yoke does when used by a farmer.

The farmer has a plough, ox or horse, and themselves. How are they to connect these three things together in order to plough the field? If the field isn't ploughed, crops can't be sown and the farmer and family will go hungry – so it's vital that the three are connected.

The answer is to use a yoke. The yoke connects the farmer, the plough and the horse together such that although they're still three, now they are also one, and the field can be ploughed and a crop sown.

What a brilliant piece of technology the yoke must have been, for no matter how strong the ox, skilled the farmer or sharp the plough, none of them can get the field ploughed without the yoke that connects them together

The three must become one by "coming together" – another translation of yuj.

In essence, that's yoga.

There are other more subtle understandings of how to interpret yoga which are also worth considering.

The great Yoga teacher T.K.V. Desikachar writes "a further meaning of the word yoga is to attain what was previously unattainable",[1] which is a brilliant insight when we once again consider the example above.

The farmer, standing in his field, looking at the size of it, and his horse, and his plough puts his head in his hands and cries "how am I going to get this done?" Linking them together enables him to attain what was previously unattainable.

Desikachar also shows that yoga can be understood as how, when we link our thoughts and our actions together, we get things done. When we're very attentive to the task in hand, when we focus all of our attention on the work before us, we're much more likely to enjoy both the work and the end result.

Here's an example of yoga in action on the sports field:

Many of us may have watched professional Rugby, perhaps on the television. After a "try" is scored, the kicker has the opportunity to score a "conversion", by kicking the ball over the opposing team's crossbar. This is a very tricky thing to do and requires a great deal of skill and attention. You may have noticed how the kicker stands perfectly still before the ball and traces its imaginary flight from his feet, through the air, and over the crossbar. You will have seen how he slowly moves his head back and forth, tracing the line with his eyes – all of his senses are absolutely engaged in the work of kicking the ball over the crossbar. Even the crowd of many thousands are completely silent while he does this. What you're seeing is yoga – the ball, the crossbar, and the kicker, even the crowd of thousands of individuals, momentarily become one.

I'm quite sure you've also seen this in many other sports – tennis and golf are two clear examples, and of course all of the great writers and artists practise the linking of their bodies and minds to their given art. The very greatest achieve their greatness due to their ability to carry out this linking in ways others have not been able to achieve. As Desikachar said, yoga can enable what was previously thought unattainable to become attainable.

Finally, Desikachar turns his attention to God when he says "another classic definition of yoga is to be one with the divine. When we feel in harmony with that higher power, that too is yoga".

As Christians we can surely understand what he means by this, we can get a glimpse of how yoga helps to move our hearts towards God, toward Divine Love.

And so yoga isn't just that class of people who turn up at the village hall on a Wednesday night and go through an hour of gentle postures, or the young people on the TV who glide through impossible looking postures with grace and ease. Not that there's anything wrong with these – both are commendable, but that's only the very surface of what yoga is about. It's like saying Christianity is about singing hymns or going to Church on a Sunday – both may be true, but it hardly touches the depths of such an ancient religion.

Perhaps you can see now why the words yoke and yoga are very similar, and that replacing one with another can throw fresh light onto Jesus's words, such that something new is revealed. Bearing in mind just some of the definitions of yoga mentioned above, you may catch a glimpse of how replacing the word yoke with yoga can charge Jesus's words with new and exciting meaning.

Practice 1
Meditation on the text

Sit with a straight back, feet flat on the floor if you're on a chair, feeling alert but relaxed.

Allow your arms to rest in your lap, or on your thighs, palms facing up if possible.

Lower your eyes and gently rest their gaze a few feet in front of you – or close them, but not tightly.

Have the text near enough to be able to read it, or try to remember it.

Take a few moments, perhaps a minute or so, to engage with (become attentive to) your breath.

Simply "watch" it, notice how it moves your body, its rhythm of ebb and flow.

Notice how it feels – perhaps slow and deep, or fast and shallow, perhaps smooth or a bit ragged.

We'll be looking into breath and breathing in more detail later, but for now just be gently attentive to how it is at the present moment.

When you're ready, read or remember the text – it's okay to whisper it to yourself, sometimes that can be very helpful. Repeat it, perhaps in harmony with your breath so that a gentle rhythm of breath and word arises. Pause momentarily at the commas or full stops – allow the sentence to sink into you – become steeped in it.

As you sit don't think too hard, simply see what arises in your mind without judgement, and pay attention to any sensations in the body, or emotions that arise.

Just be open to their arising and *experience* the text, rather than trying to understand it.

> Come unto me all who are weary and heavy laden, and I will give you rest.
> Take my yoga upon you and learn of me, for I am gentle and humble in heart,
> And you will find rest in your souls
> For my yoga is easy, and my burden is light..

When you've completed this meditation (take as long as you like over it) you may like to place your hands together in the prayer mudra (mudra just means symbolic hand gesture), and placing them in the region of your heart in the middle of the chest, make a little bow.

I'm aware we don't bow much in Christianity, mostly because we've some odd ideas about what bowing means, however, in the East it's mostly an action of humility and gratitude. So if you'd like to, simply bow in gratitude and thanks for Jesus's words. They are, after all, life-changing.

Chapter 1

To Follow Is to Practise Yoga

At the beginning of Jesus's ministry, all four gospels record Jesus as saying "follow me" to those he'd chosen to be his students (Mathew 4.19, Mark 1.17, Luke 5.27, John 1.43).

This call wasn't simply to casually tag along behind and see what happens next, but a life-changing call to be a full-time disciple. This isn't new to Jesus but was a typical Eastern tradition. Disciples would leave their homes and employment and live with their Master, Teacher or Guru for many years – in India 12 years was considered the least amount of time to commit. It's interesting to note that the words disciple and discipline have the same root – one infers the other.

The point is that this is a call to live in intimate relationship with the Teacher. The student would learn from their teacher and also look after their needs. Through finding and preparing food, resting, sleeping, speaking, singing or chanting together, sitting in silence or simply experiencing everyday life together, the student would quite literally "follow" the Master into each day as it unfolded.

In this way the Master's teaching is not confined to the classroom or interesting talks, courses or books, but the whole of life becomes a text – not to be taught but to be lived.

The Master, the disciple, and all of life, become intimately linked, yoked together – united in their love and respect for one another as they encounter the vicissitudes of life.

For Jesus to call his disciples and ask them to bear his yoke, is not so much to do with Jesus somehow steering his disciples (we often mistake the text for an offer of Jesus to "steer" us through life – particularly when it's not going the way we'd like). It's more to do with living in intimate relationship – yoked together. This is a call to experience first-hand the yoga of Jesus, the way he was with people, events, the natural world, friends, enemies, Government, Religion, being hungry and thirsty, encountering danger, sadness and joy.

Perhaps you can begin to glimpse how using the word yoga, rather than yoke, opens up the possibilities of discovering a new and more profound understanding of Jesus's life and of following him more attentively.

More even than this, the term yoke is quite passive – yoked animals only go where they're led – there's no need to think much, just follow the pull of the reins. Much religion is unfortunately received like this – many people feel they're not really required to think or do much, but rather receive what is being taught, believe it, and carry on. Bible study is often done with the use of "Bible notes" and Commentary, so we can look at what the experts say in order to see if we're on the right track. We not asked to think too much, and serious questioning is often not encouraged – we might even feel guilty for forming a question that others see as a weakness in our faith. As a Retreat Leader and Spiritual Director, I've met countless Christians and seekers who have sadly experienced this. Perhaps you have too.

To follow Jesus is to practise life

Yoga on the other hand requires us to deeply consider, and then to act. It doesn't contain any doctrine or dogma. It requires experience, practice and reflection. The Sanskrit word for this is *abhyasa,* or sometimes *sadhana*. In order for us to better understand what these words mean, we need to let go of our usual Western understanding of the term "practice" (think of the noun preparation). In the West we mostly associate it with sporadic times of focussed activity, that is, we practise (think of the verb to prepare) the piano for an hour each day, or our golf swing at the weekend, and so on.

Abhyasa is nothing like that. Abhyasa means constant practice, it's a way of life – every moment is practice, not just a few hours each week. If you can count the hours you've been practising, that's not abhyasa.

The nearest we get in the West to this understanding is its use in some of the professions. For example, doctors and dentists have a "practice" and so do lawyers. We all know this doesn't mean these people have announced that they're still not properly qualified and need to improve themselves! Rather, it means a total commitment to their work, a "profession" of their life to a particular discipline – almost "a way of life".

The very first "professionals" of course, were Monks.

Yoga requires practice, or it isn't yoga. Our relationships (with everything) need to be practised in order for us to realise the truth about them, and so to have, as Jesus puts it, "life abundantly".[2]

Practice in this sense is to live with the intention of encountering the truth as each day, each moment arises. Why would we want to live in any other way? Living a deluded life is deeply unsatisfactory, which in turn creates vast amounts of suffering, and yet most of us never practise our lives but simply receive what comes along with varying amounts of pleasure or grief. To follow Jesus, to take his yoga and learn of him, is to practise our lives in accordance with what we see and hear of him. He arose in humanity in order to enable us to break through our delusions, not add to them, and the only way to do that is to understand our entire lives as practice, as he did.

This needn't cause us any worries, however, because unlike the Western understanding of practice, this has nothing to do with getting better at something, measuring ourselves against some external standard and feeling happy or dismayed as a result. This mistake includes using Jesus's life as a measuring rod. For as many years as I can remember, in my own Church-going and from the majority of Christian texts and liturgies I've studied, this is what Christians often feel burdened with.

Apparently, we have to be good as Jesus is good, to be like him whom the Church proclaims is God and therefore perfect. The Church has a particular model of what it means by "perfect", as do many other religions, and it's a standard that no human can possibly achieve.

Therefore, people are seen to "fail" (sin) and are required to confess their "failures" over and over again – and although these are forgiven, by the time most of us have reached the Church door to go home, we've failed again!

In fact, the religious rhythm of much Christianity (and other religions) is one of failure and forgiveness – on and on it goes, endlessly. Finally, when we die, (and the human being is at its most vulnerable), we arrive before the judgement seat of "Almighty" God, who may give us the green light to eternal life, or pronounce something very much worse.

I'm aware there are many shades of that process, but essentially that's how it goes.

But Jesus says "you will find rest for your souls, for my yoga is easy and my burden light".

If there is a standard to be measured, it is simply this – how united do you feel to your life and the life unfolding all around you?

Are you increasingly happy and content (at rest) in your deepest sense of self?

Are you at peace with your neighbours – all of them, including the animals, insects, and plants?

Most people aren't at peace with the weather, let alone their troublesome neighbours. The only yardstick by which we can tell if our practice is helping, is that offered by Jesus: "Love the Lord your God with all your heart and with all your soul, and with all your mind." This is the greatest and first commandment. And a second is like it: "You shall love your neighbour as yourself. On these two commandments hang all the law and the prophets."[3]

To love God, neighbour and self is the purpose of the practice of life, but there's no score card and no one is keeping count. This kind of practice isn't about winning or losing, failing or succeeding, it's simply about fulfilling our God-given life, "having life to the full, or abundantly" just as we are, right here right now.

And we know when that's on track, or if we're temporarily de-railed because we feel it – we know when we're suffering and when we're not, and suffering is always to do with love and trust (faith), or the lack thereof. People can accommodate the most awful suffering when they're being loved through it – I'm sure you already know that.

Jesus's call to follow him and take his yoga upon you, is his call to give and receive love as he does. It's as simple as that.

The question then arises, how to do that?

There are many ways, but in the end the most effective are all forms of yoga – the uniting of what appears to be separate such that we might "attain what seemed previously unattainable". The greatest example of this in the Bible is the moment Jesus says from the cross, "Father, forgive them for they do not know what they're doing."[4]

And lest anyone think that this path of yoga has something to do with personal will, it doesn't. It's to do with grace. Sure enough, we have to commit to the path, we need to make an effort, but just like the prodigal son discovered,[5] take one step toward home and home takes ten steps toward us. It's always waiting for us on the edge of our delusion – that's the way divine love works.

Chapter 2

The Four Yogas of Jesus

For most people in the West, yoga has to do with exercise and postures – the kind of thing we see on the front of magazines or on YouTube channels. Others who go to yoga classes know a little more – that yoga also has to do with breathing techniques, and perhaps even quiet meditation. We shall come back to these in a while. Yoga though, is multi-stranded, very subtle, and offers many ways to engage with it. Just as Christianity and most other religions offer different expressions, yoga also has different paths. Unlike most religious traditions though, these paths are not offered in competition with, or as alternatives to the others – the paths of yoga are complementary to one another. There are times in our lives when things are going in a certain direction for us, and at other times a change arises and so our direction changes too – in other words life is seasonal and dynamic. Yoga respects this – humans are not static entities but constantly flowing and changing both within and without. Take a look at a photograph of yourself from just five years ago, remember what life was like then, what your priorities were, what was really important to you, what your most precious relationships were, and you'll know what I'm talking about. Life flows.

I've already mentioned that yoga has to do with our relationships with everything, the "yoking"of ourselves to our entire lives, and yoga flows as our life flows. The beauty is that it provides us with both stability (*sthira* in Sanskrit), and ease/ comfort (*sukha*), helping us to navigate whatever new terrain we're encountering. More on this aspect of yoga later.

Yoga has many forms but there are four which are highly significant, and the Bible shows how Jesus practises all of them (remember practice doesn't mean trying to get better at them, it means living them).

In no particular order, the four yoga's are:

Jnana yoga: The yoga of knowledge. This has to do with realising (making real) the truth of how things actually are, not what we think they are, or would like them to be. It includes but isn't confined to what we'd normally consider to be knowledge, (subjective information) as jnana yoga transcends cerebral ideas. It's a knowledge based not solely on rational thought but centred on profound *experience* such that rational knowledge alone dissolves into inadequacy. For Christians this would be the knowledge, for example, that nothing "will be able to separate us from the love of God".[6] Not because we believe it (somebody told us, or we read it) but because we know it through experience, even if that experience is fleeting. It's "gut" based knowledge, born of experiencing such love even when rational explanations might say something very different, for example, the experience of the person who wrote on a cellar wall during WW2, "I believe in the sun even when it is not shining, I believe in love even when I cannot feel it. I believe in God even when he is silent."

Jesus's "knowledge" of God didn't come from long hours of studying scriptures in the academic sense, although it's very clear he did study and understand the scriptures. But even at an early age he was able to discuss profound ideas of God with the academics of his day,[7] and later on as an adult, Jesus's knowledge was clearly different from the usual, "and they were astounded at his teaching, because he spoke with authority."[8] This authority was a natural consequence of Jesus's deep inner experience, not the result of abstract academic study or simply believing what he'd been told. This kind of knowledge, jnana, is available to all humans should they desire it enough. It requires an enquiring mind not content with someone else's answers or ideas, but desiring to look more deeply into Life. Working with rational knowledge but more importantly experiential knowledge, the authenticity of what is actually the case (the "Truth", not an abstract), is the practice of jnana yoga. Jesus certainly possessed this kind of knowledge and practised this kind of yoga.

Bhakti Yoga: The yoga of devotion to God. Of the four yoga's, this is the one most associated with Religion. Bhakti yoga is to be so devoted to God that we lose our self-centred lives and live only in service and worship of the Lord. It's the yoga of devoted love for God and everything that God loves, and so is the yoga of participation in the life and love of God. It is to serve, honour, worship and adore. It's the yoga of deepest intimacy. We see examples of this in all the great theistic faiths and certainly within the Christian tradition, for example, within the mysticism of Dame Julian of Norwich,[9] or even St Francis of Assisi who was so devoted to Jesus that he received stigmata.[10] Jesus, however, never asked for such devotion from his disciples, they were only asked to follow him and believe their experiences. As time went by it was out of personal experience of Jesus that devotion naturally arose in them, as it can do with anyone who cultivates such a relationship with Jesus today, albeit in a different way.

Jesus's yoga (remember yoga means to unify) was such that he was able to say "you may know and understand that the Father is in me, and I am in the Father".[11] Not only that, his devotion to God included within it his devotion to his disciples, such that he was also able to say, "the glory that you have given me I have given them, so that they may be one, as we are one; I in them and you in me, that they may become completely one."[12] Finally, Jesus's actions even more than his words, are eloquent enough witness to his devotion to God, his practice of Bhakti yoga. This is a constant theme throughout the gospels, from healing on the Sabbath (against Jewish Law of the time), to forgiving the "woman caught in adultery", right until his "Passion" which Christians celebrate in Holy Week.

What we should take note of, however, is that Bhakti yoga – loving devotion to God, also included loving the disciples, loving people of other faith traditions (Greeks, Romans, Samaritans) and even enemies. Indeed, all humanity. Jesus's love of God cannot be separated from his love for humanity – it's the same thing and he makes that very clear when he says to "Love your enemies, pray for those who persecute you",[13] "Love the Lord your God with all your heart, and with all your soul, and with all your mind, and with all your strength" and "Love your neighbour as yourself".[14] That scripture in itself is a perfect explanation of the outworking of Bhakti yoga.

Karma Yoga: The yoga of selfless action. This is action focussed entirely on the work at hand and devoid of any desire for reward or return. In the third chapter of the great Indian spiritual work the Bhagavad Gita, karma yoga – the yoga of "selfless service" – is fully explained. It goes on to say, "at the beginning, humankind and the obligation of selfless service were created together. Through selfless service, you will always be fruitful and find the fulfilment of your desires: this is the promise of the Creator."[15] In the Bible we have a similar verse attributed to Jesus: "But strive first for the kingdom of God and his righteousness, and all these things will be given to you as well."[16]

We might even see how karma yoga is beautifully elucidated in the great Christian prayer, "Lord teach me to be generous, teach me to serve you as you deserve, to give and not to count the cost; To fight and not to heed the wounds; To toil, and not to seek for rest; To labour, and not to ask for reward – except to know that I am doing your will."[17]

This is a prayer for the gift of karma yoga – the gift of selfless service. We might see how it also touches on Bhakti yoga too – the yoga of complete devotion to the Lord.

When Jesus called the disciples, he said "follow me", and the disciples "left their nets" and followed him.[18] From that first selfless action, the disciples would be confronted again and again by the uncompromising karma yoga of Jesus, always and only seeking to do his Father's will, which was entirely centred on the salvation of humankind, no matter what the cost. The Cross, of course, is the epitome of Jesus's practice of karma yoga.

Raja Yoga: The yoga of meditation and prayer. Raja is a Sanskrit word meaning "King", so we might understand this as "Royal Yoga" – the most important of the yoga practices. For most Christians, prayer is something we do for fairly short amounts of time, and is very often of the discursive kind – that is, we use words. Whether prayers of intercession (asking God for something on behalf of others) or thanksgiving, or worship, or confession, our prayers usually last only a few minutes and are articulated through words – whether we speak them with our lips, or with our minds. Raja yoga is more akin to Christian meditation and contemplation – which is wordless, or uses very few words, and often lasts for long periods, anything from 20 minutes to several hours on a regular basis.

In other words, this kind of prayer requires discipline and levels of commitment that very few Christians know much about or engage in. Yet it is precisely this kind of prayer that Jesus practised, regularly going out into deserted places and mountainsides before dawn to sit quietly in solitude. Perhaps the best example of this in the Bible is immediately after Jesus's baptism by John, when "immediately the Spirit compelled him to go out into the wilderness"[19] alone for 40 days.

Jesus says this concerning prayer: "When you pray, you are not to be like the hypocrites; for they love to stand and pray in the synagogues, and on the street corners so that they may be seen by men. Truly, I say to you they have their reward in full. But you, when you pray, go into your room and shut the door, and pray to your Father who is in secret."[20] This inner "room" where the Father resides in secret, isn't simply a physical space within a building, but refers to our deepest sense of self – our "hearts". This inner chamber is the quiet place that all budding contemplatives intuit lies within them, even if they don't have the language to articulate it. To enter this room and to close the door, is to enter the silence of that inner space and close the "door" of our chattering minds and restless thoughts. That may well be best achieved by physically moving into a quiet room and closing an actual door, but essentially it means entering the heart of God. Rather than endless repetitive word-prayers that eventually just run into the sand, (prayers for every occasion), Jesus offers us a prayer practice that has become known to us as "the Lord's prayer". The way we're to practise this, is once the prayer is said (and notice how short it is), the idea is to become quiet and allow it to do its internal work. Reading chapters 6 and 7 of Matthew's gospel will give you a good insight into the beginnings of Christian "Raja" yoga, and how Jesus practised.

In yoga, this practice is understood to be an "heroic" spiritual undertaking, precisely because it's so difficult to maintain, and yet it's this practice which has the most astonishing and transformative effect – and I speak here from personal experience (and I'm definitely not in the least bit heroic).

Christianity has a wonderful and long tradition of meditation and contemplative prayer, but sadly, this has been much neglected for many hundreds of years. The wisdom and traditions of the Desert Fathers and Mothers of the third century, the Cappadocian Fathers, St Benedict, St Francis, St Hilda of Bingen, Dame Julian of Norwich, St Theresa of Avila, St Catherine of Genoa, St John of the Cross, the Celtic Fathers and Mothers, and many others, have been largely consigned to the margins of Christianity until only very recently. In the modern era, beginning with Thomas Merton in the 1950s, the wisdom and practice of Christian contemplative prayer has been revived by people such as John Main, Cynthia Bourgeault, Thomas Keating, Richard Rohr, and more teachers arising all the time, as this ancient and honourable practice is breathed into new life. It seems its time has come – and the fact that you've picked this book to read indicates that you too are part of the new arising of that ancient wisdom. Jesus's practice of Raja yoga was fundamental to his ability to say what he said and do what he did.

Summary and practice

When Jesus said "follow me" and proclaimed that his yoga was easy and provided souls with rest, he was asking us to watch him very attentively – how he was with everything – and do likewise.

He wasn't speaking about theology, doctrines and dogmas that in years, in some cases centuries later, people (mostly men) would create in order to try and explain him. Jesus's teaching ministry (he was known as Rabbi – teacher) was simply to invite people to be with him as he encountered life in all its diversity, difficulty and joy – to see his relationships at work, and to do likewise.

We can see how we might recognise at least four elements of yoga in his life, Jnana yoga – the way of wisdom, Bhakti yoga – the way of loving devotion, Karma yoga – the way of selfless action, and Raja yoga – the way of meditation and contemplative prayer. We might call these the "Four Yogas of Jesus", and in taking up his yoke (yoga), we commit ourselves to practising these in our lives too. This is what it means (at the very least) to follow Jesus.

Practices

- Re-read the four yogas and consider which of these is the one that first attracted you to be a disciple of Jesus – or if you don't identify with being a Christian as such, which do you find most inspiring?
- Select one of the yogas and consider how you might practise it during the next 7 days. Perhaps keep a journal – write how you've been practising your chosen yoga. After 7 days reflect on the experience. Perhaps you felt you followed Jesus a little more closely over the period, or maybe you felt a bit better about yourself or others. Maybe it was just frustrating?
- Read a gospel, or a few chapters at least, and see if you can identify Jesus's yogas in action. Are they easily identifiable, perhaps they merge into one another and are hard to segment? Yoga, the action and experience of being united (whole) is in the end "all of a piece", with no beginning or end, so not to worry if it's hard to separate one from another.

Chapter 3

The Body of Yoga Has Eight Limbs

Limb 1 Yama: (How to be with each other)

As I hope you can see now, yoga itself is not a religion but a way of being in the world that can help both people of faith and those without a commitment to any particular religion. Yoga is sometimes called the "science of religion" as its approach to life is very practical and based on the experience of being human. Yogis are not asked to believe anything – just practise yoga and see for themselves.

Classical yoga as expressed by Patanjali[21] in his "Yoga Sutra", comprises of eight different but interconnected aspects, which Patanjali calls "limbs" (*ashtanga* = 8 limbs).

The majority of the rest of this book is dedicated to looking at each of these and relating them to Christian thought where it seems natural and appropriate. If you're a person of faith (either Christian or otherwise) you may start to make your own connections – which is an exciting experience, and a great encouragement to your own spiritual maturation.

The first two limbs of yoga are to do with its codes of ethics. Most Westerners have no idea that yoga has such codes, probably because it's seen and practised mostly as an aid to physical health and mental wellbeing. Certainly, most Christians know nothing of its ethical codes, particularly those who consign yoga to merely occult practices that should be avoided. Yet these codes form the first two limbs, which in Indian tradition of scripture-writing mean they're the most important and the context within which the rest of the writing should be seen.

For those of us who take our yoga practice seriously, the rest of the limbs – all of our postures (*asana*), breathing (*pranayama*) working with our senses (*pratyahara*) and meditation (*dharana* /

dhyana / samadhi) – should be helping us to realise these first two limbs: The *Yama* and the *Niyama*.

Yama literally means restraint and is about how we interact with the "outside" world. There are five Yamas:

1. Non-harming/non-violence/without cruelty (*ahimsa*)
2. Truthfulness/honesty (*satya*)
3. Non-stealing (*asteya)*
4. Fidelity towards the truth (*brahmacarya*)
5. Non-grasping/greedlessness (*aprigraha*)

As can be seen, these moral obligations are not so very different to what Christians find in "the ten commandments" or indeed codes of ethics within many religions and faiths. In yoga they constitute "the great vow" (*maha-vrata),* in other words these aren't simply a set of commandments to keep or face punishment, or even a nice idea to work towards, but a *deep personal commitment on how to live our life*.

We shall now pause to reflect on each of them more deeply, and after each one there's an invitation to take the Yama for oneself, and if you feel able and willing, to make the vow.

Ahimsa

Ahimsa is the opposite of *himsa*, which means violence, injustice, cruelty and so on. The prefix "a" in front of any Sanskrit word means the opposite of ... so Ahimsa is the opposite of himsa. We may take this to be an injunction against acting unjustly, violently or cruelly toward another person, and just as importantly towards oneself. But it means much more than that. Ahimsa calls us toward looking deeply into our relationships with all beings everywhere and seeing the subtlety of how we can act violently and cruelly without even noticing it. We know it's not right to engage in violence against another human, and we may have a notion that it's not right to treat animals cruelly either. However, we may think nothing of killing slugs and snails with poisonous pellets, or spraying "weeds" with chemicals. We may let a butterfly out of our home if it flies in by mistake but think nothing of crushing a fly's fragile body with a fly-swat, or hoovering up a spider. Keeping chickens or other animals in small cages or even large barns with no access to natural sunlight, the breeze, natural sounds and experiences are forms of violence.

Violence can be even more subtle. Our speech can be violent, using words designed to inflict harm on others, and harbouring or enjoying thoughts of retribution and fantasising about "getting our own back", even if we have no intention of actually doing so. Even harbouring ideas about others that are tantamount to prejudice, are forms of violence – they're violent because they're injurious to the other even though it's an injury that only occurs in our heads. Violence is violence, and such violent thoughts always injure the thinker too as they create scars in our own hearts and minds.

Ahimsa is a state of mind, not just the avoidance of causing physical harm. It's a way of being in the world that takes account of the suffering of ALL creatures EVERYWHERE. Just because the creature is not a favourite of ours, or perhaps is a non-sentient being (like a mountain or river), doesn't mean that we can turn our backs on their suffering. Neither have we the right to decide if the being is suffering or not, simply because we don't think they do. Slugs suffer terribly when we poison them, ants suffer terribly when we pour boiling water over their nests, and mountains suffer in the ways mountains do when we reduce them to rubble looking for copper, tin or gold.

Ahimsa is the state of mind that sees the possibility of violence, injustice and cruelty being inflicted on any Being, and takes the opposite course of action to reduce or remove its suffering.

Even if we are placed in a situation that requires us to take an action likely to kill or injure another being (for example, in self-defence or defending the weak or defence-less) ahimsa requires the minimal force to be used and do what needs to be done in full knowledge of the gravity of our action. Violence is avoided or undertaken reluctantly with full consideration of the consequences – in every situation we adopt a considered attitude which arises naturally as we practise living a life of ahimsa.

It's clear that the practice of ahimsa was a central tenet of Jesus's life. The beatitudes carry the weight of ahimsa, as do his commandments to "turn the other cheek", and "love your enemies, do good to those who hate you".[22] His behaviour during his torture, trial and execution are exemplary acts of ahimsa, and on his resurrection he never advocated any form of violence towards those who had acted so violently toward him – indeed he practised the complete inverse.

Finally, in the Indian tradition, opening and closing statements carry more weight than those in-between, and the commentators of the Yoga Sutra are quick to point out that ahimsa is the first of the yamas. In this sense then, ahimsa is the yama to which all of the following yamas are subject – it is both the context and the goal of what comes next.

Invitation

Spend a short time considering when you've been the victim of violence, and how it made you feel. Consider the times you've perpetrated violence on another. Be kind to yourself as you consider these things – don't fall into either guilt or anger. If you feel ready, make a vow to practise Ahimsa. Make the vow using your own words, or another way that means something to you – either to God, Jesus, the Universe, or just to your deepest sense of self. Notice how you feel afterward and notice any opportunities to practise ahimsa in the following days.

Satya

This means truthfulness, to practise the truth. Truth is seen by all religious traditions as supremely important, which is why the great Indian politician and religious leader Mahatma Gandhi was able to say, "Truth is God and God is Truth." In the Christian tradition truth is no less important, with some of Jesus's most well-known sayings containing a reference, for example, "I am the way, and the truth and the life",[23] or "and you will know the truth and the truth will make you free".[24]

Truth is a tricky subject because it's not always clear what is true and what is not. In the Buddhist tradition, truth can be seen as either relative or absolute, which can be helpful. For example, we might say that the sun rises in the East and sets in the West. That's true, but only relatively so – it's only true if one is standing on the earth. Absolutely speaking, the sun doesn't move at all, but the earth's rotation makes it appear to do so. So the statement is relatively true, but not absolutely. Absolute truth therefore includes relative truth, but isn't defined or contained by it, whereas relative truth is always dependent on circumstances.

Truth isn't limited to the words we speak, although we often associate truth with things that are said (or not said). Neither is it confined to our actions although we rarely consider whether or not our actions are truthful. How might we act un-truthfully? Maybe we believe that climate change is destroying the earth but do little or nothing to change our own behaviour? When our beliefs or commitments don't manifest in our actions, that's not practising satya.

For truth to manifest, speech, actions and thoughts have to be in alignment, they need to interlace each other and uphold one other. In other words, they need to express unity. There's no room for gaps or fragmentation when it comes to truth, truth is always a unified whole, which is precisely why Mahatma

Gandhi was able to say God is Truth and Truth is God (indeed the title of his autobiography is *God Is Truth*).

God cannot be other than Truth, and cannot be other than whole – anything less on either part and it's not of God.

So to practise satya in our lives is no small thing. Even a cursory look into our own behaviour will reveal the fact that we're far from truthful in all sorts of ways. We may well find too that this untruthfulness contributes a great deal to our own unhappiness or sense of isolation. It plays a significant part in feelings of frustration with life, guilt, anger and hurt. However, Jesus says "the truth will set you free", and that's because non-truth always holds us back. It stops us from realising our beautiful true selves, and the beautiful true selves of others, stuck as we are in the fog of delusion. Now I know seeking, finding and admitting truth can seem a fearful thing to do, which is one reason we may not pursue it. So it calls for courage, and in particular faith (that is trust) that God is to be found wherever truth is to be found. The "Way" is synonymous with the "Truth" according to Jesus, and in fact, both are the very stuff of "Life".

So we need not be afraid of Truth, because it's the very presence of God, who remember, is Love.

In the yoga tradition, however, there's a very important caveat to satya (and indeed all the eight limbs of yoga). Remember that it's second in the list of Yamas, the first and most important being ahimsa. Truth therefore must serve non-harming. Satya should never undermine or come into conflict with ahimsa, that is, if the pursuit of truth creates violence and harm, it needs very careful consideration – particularly around the motivation for it. Satya is not legalism, it's very important to understand that. Satya is Love. Any other motivation for satya is a corruption of it. In this way, the yogic concept of satya is in perfect alignment with the Christian understanding of Love. As Joseph Fletcher writes "the ruling norm of Christian religion is love: nothing else".[25] Provided satya is practised in the light of Love, then it will be fulfilling its purpose.

Invitation

Consider the place of truth in your life; how truth-full is it, how integrated in speech, thought and action? In what ways might you be avoiding truth, and how might these be hurting you or someone you love?

Remember that according to Jesus "the truth will set you free", so be careful with the motivation around your work with satya – its only purpose is the fulfilling of Love – if it doesn't do that, it needs deeper understanding and maybe setting aside for a time while you work on it. Satya is not legalism but Love.

When you feel ready, make a vow to practise Satya. Make the vow using your own words, or another way that means something to you – either to God, Jesus, the Universe, or just to your deepest sense of self. Notice how you feel afterward and notice any opportunities to practise satya in the following days.

Asteya

Asteya is the third yama, meaning not to steal. Taking something which is not ours, which doesn't belong to us, is stealing, however, there are many levels of theft and yoga invites us to look deeply into them.

Most people know that taking what does not belong to us isn't right, but we tend to limit this to objects, "things". We know it's not right to steal another's mobile phone, car or wallet, but what about relationships? To sabotage someone else's relationship in order that we might possess it, is stealing (note, for example, the song "Joline" by American Country singer Dolly Parton). Neither is it right to steal someone else's time by either outstaying our welcome, keeping them talking too long, or borrowing something and not returning it.

Misusing things is also a form of theft, that is, using things in ways which harm them or cause them damage.

Using animals as weapons (for example, training dogs to kill or injure people or dolphins to carry mines) steals their true nature and is a terrible theft of their integrity. Taking more than we need is also theft. I don't suppose they realised it but those who emptied the shelves in supermarkets during the early days of the coronavirus pandemic, leaving nothing for others, were committing theft as understood in this yama, even though they paid for their items at the till. Had they known that, and practised asteya, there would have been enough toilet rolls, pasta and bread for everyone.

Another level of theft is that of taking life. Not that anyone reading this book has probably intentionally taken a human life, but most will have killed flies, wasps, slugs etc., because they're "pests", or you're afraid of them. However, all life is God-given and none has the right to steal it from another, particularly for such self-centred reasons as personal dislike. In this case, theft is very closely related to violence, and in fact yoga makes a direct connection between theft and violence because it always sees stealing as a violent act.

The current climate crisis is caused by the most terrible acts of theft as humans rob the earth (and so all its creatures including other humans) of its minerals, plants, animals, seas, fresh water, clean air, and so on. This is both grand theft and great violence, both of which we have yet to see the full consequences of.

We are also very good at stealing each other's nature. Every time we take a "view" of someone, decide on whether they fit our preferred idea of what looks good or bad, cool or un-cool or deride their hair colour, clothes, accent, skin colour, home-town or country, or do the opposite – when we want someone because they make us feel good about ourselves (e.g., "celebrity" culture), that is all theft. Finally, the greatest and most subtle theft of all, is the theft of ourselves. When we live self-centred lives and reference everything else to the tiny world of "me", we steal ourselves away from the great family into which we've been born. Removing ourselves from our cosmic family and being estranged from our brothers and sisters (see St Francis), to live fearful solitary lives in competition with everyone and everything else, is the most subtle and terrible theft of all. It's a theft whose consequences are played out in the most awful of ways, filled with personal and corporate tragedy, as the countless feuds, wars, family rifts, and personal sufferings testify. Once again stealing is accompanied by violence. This theft of the self, of course, is ultimately a theft from God for we are not our own, we didn't arise into life by our own efforts, we cannot sustain our life by our own efforts, and we cannot avoid our deaths by our own efforts. To have "life to the full" as Jesus says, is to know this deeply for ourselves. Prayer of course is the antidote to the theft of the self as it keeps us connected to the one from whom our life proceeds. Prayer therefore is at the heart of the practice of asteya with the ultimate realisation that in God we have everything we need, and so any desire we have to steal, ceases.

Invitation

Consider the many ways in which you take what does not belong to you. We all do this, as theft is much more subtle than just taking a chocolate bar from a shop without paying, so there's no need to feel awkward or defensive when you consider the issue. Perhaps make a list and spend a little time with it – you might discover a pattern of behaviour. After a while you might like to offer prayers of repentance, saying sorry for unintentional harms done, and know surely that you're forgiven. Make a commitment to practise asteya by looking out for the subtle ways of theft, and avoiding them. To help you make the connection between asteya and ahimsa, that is not stealing on any level, makes the world a much kinder and less violent place.

Brahmacarya

Translated literally this means "movement toward God" (Brahman, the Absolute), however, it's often translated as celibacy or abstention from sexual activity. In classical yoga, the yogis of old didn't marry but gave themselves entirely to the pursuit of spiritual practice and union with the divine, therefore celibacy was a clear indication of their "movement toward God". Later on, when yoga became something that "householders" could practise rather than the reserve of monks or nuns, Brahmacarya became a call to thoughtful and considerate sexual relationships within the context of marriage rather than abstinence. To withhold sexual intimacy from a partner in marriage without their consent because "now I'm a yogi" (for example), is understood as theft, so breaking the yama and the very thing looking to be achieved.

Brahmacarya can also be understood as "fidelity to the Truth" or movement towards Truth through self-control and conscious moderation of our instincts. It's the ability to channel our desires, impulses and longings toward a higher goal than self-gratification, be they sexual or any other inclinations, such as eating too much or drinking alcohol, for example. If we are serious about the goal of yoga, that is, the realisation of union with the Divine, then the practice of Brahmacarya is critical if we're not to get side-tracked down the dead ends of desire and impulse, wasting precious time and energy.

Invitation

Does it feel that your life is a movement towards God, or your deepest sense of self, or something else? How would you describe your path – a straight line, a zigzag, going round in circles, perhaps even going backwards? How in control of your impulses and desires are you? Look into the matter and see – you'll probably find that in some areas you're very able to resist particular desires, whereas other impulses are harder to avoid.

Be kind to yourself as you look into the matter, this isn't a "witch hunt" but a gentle look at where you might be wasting precious time and energy running down roads of desire that constantly end up in dead ends. If you see a pattern of behaviour, become aware of it when it arises and seek to avoid going down the rabbit hole by employing diversionary tactics that keep you on track. The more you practise the better you become at not getting lost in impulse, however, it's very important to know that desires and impulses can be hard to break and may take some considerable time. It may be that finding some support in the way of a trusted friend can be helpful. Either way, what is most important is always to be kind to oneself, practising ahimsa on the self is as equally important as practising it for others. As in the previous Yamas, if you feel able to, make a commitment to Brahmacarya. For Christians it's the same thing as following the Way.

Aparigraha

The last of the five Yamas literally means "do not seize" or "hands-off". *Parigraha* means to seize or to grab, so *Aparigraha* is the exact opposite – don't be grasping.

Georg Feuerstein writes "in a way, this is the perfect form of non-stealing".[26]

This is particularly so when cultivated (like all the Yamas) as an attitude of mind. It's the complete absence of want, or a disinterest in the acquisition of anything. This isn't confined simply to physical objects such as mobile phones, cars or clothes, but also to status, relationships, experiences or even belief systems. To the yogi such grasping (parigraha) shows a fundamental mistrust in God's providence, a lack of both faith and self-control (remember self-control is one of the "fruits of the spirit".[27] How can we focus on realising our unity with God and indeed all beings everywhere, when we're constantly on the lookout for something else, something better, something to make us feel important, special or even more real.

Grasping can be used to distract us from our intended goal too; it's the weapon of procrastination. How many times have we set out to achieve something, found it difficult or tedious (even the thought of it!) and ended up doing something else – grasping at almost anything that comes along instead of focussing on our task. That's parigraha (grasping) in action. Then there's the idea that if we could just have a particular thing, our life would be so much better, perhaps even complete. And so we focus all our attention on grasping that particular object and we're miserable until we get it, or distraught if we don't. Experience tells us though, that even if we get the object we so desperately desire, chances are it will not satisfy us for very long – something "better" will eventually arise and our grasping mind will drop the former and go after the new "shiny" object. As is the case with objects, it could also be a job, a skill, an experience or a relationship. We can spend our entire lives in the grip of parigraha and never know it. What a tragedy that is.

To practise the opposite – Aparigraha – is to notice the craving and desire for things, the nature of grasping, but not to entertain it or "invite it to tea", as a friend of mine says. As it comes in through the front door, just open the back door and let it pass through!

Practising aparigraha is to simply see our minds at work, grasping after this or that, never really happy or content but always on the lookout for something better. Just noticing this is a huge leap forward in our understanding of ourselves. Continuing the practice involves looking more deeply into why a particular object appears so attractive, what is it trying to replace in our life? Un-clutching the hand of the mind and letting the desire pass is the most difficult part of the practice, but given time it brings a gift much greater than the desired object – *freedom*. Wide open spaces, vast potential, and deep peace are the fruits of aparigraha, all of which just can't be seen while we live in the shadow of the grasping nature.

Invitation

Sitting quietly, reflect on a time when you had an overwhelming desire for an object, or perhaps you have one now? Notice your feelings as you bring the object to mind, perhaps even your body changes (shallow breath, feeling hot or restless?). Go deeper – look into what you're hoping the object will do for you, what will it bring that you're missing at the moment? Continue to look – is it the object itself that you seek to grasp, or is it something it represents – something deeper that seems to be lacking in your life, can you name that apparent lack? Visualise the object in six months' time, then six years' time, then ten years' time – will it still have the same attraction then as now, will it still be filling the gap? Clench both hands together as if grasping it with both, then take a long slow out-breath (exhale) and gently open your hands skywards and visualise letting the object go – see it gently float away, or dissolve and feel its weight or pull, leave you.

Leave the hands open, take a long slow in-breath (inhale) and visualise receiving spaciousness, freedom, and contentedness. Know your happiness and peacefulness is not dependent on anything created by someone else, or contingent on someone else, but that you already have that which you seek – it's simply that in grasping after these other things, you've missed the exquisite nature of your true self. The Bible says you are made in the image of God – if that's true (and I believe it is), then grasping after things is like trying to make your image better in a mirror by drawing on the mirror surface. Just polish the mirror to see how truly beautiful and complete you already are. The mind is the mirror, practising aparigraha is the practice of polishing.

Chapter 4

Limb 2 Niyama: (How to Be with Ourselves)

The second "limb" of Patanjali's yoga concerns the *Niyamas*. Just as the Yamas are all about our external relationships, so the niyamas are about our inner life – how we are with ourselves, the health of our body-mind-spirit. As before there are five of these, as follows:

Saucha

Usually translated as "cleanliness" or "purity", it refers to both an outer and inner aspect. The outer aspect applies to our physical bodies in at least two ways. Firstly, there's the outer body that we can see, that is, our torso, limbs, skin, hair etc. It's obviously beneficial to keep these clean and in good order by washing and caring for them, trimming and cleaning nails, using good quality natural oils and moisturisers on the skin, protecting the eyes, ears and skin from the elements, cleaning teeth, and so on.

Secondly within the external aspect, there's the physical body that we can't see. This includes the cleanliness and purity of our internal organs – to keep them functioning well. Yoga is keen to ensure all our inner organs are maintained at their optimum level, not just heart and lungs but the brain, stomach, intestines, bowel, kidneys, liver, reproductive organs. Also our sinews, ligaments, muscles, bones, joints are all included here, along with veins and arteries. Most essentially it covers that which controls and coordinates the entire operation of our bodies – the internal communication system; our central, peripheral and sensory nervous systems are also included. Indeed, the outer aspect of shauca covers every aspect of our physical bodies, both external and internal. This is because the body is understood to be the vehicle through which our unity with the Divine is realised. If the vehicle isn't functioning well, if it's constantly "breaking down", always in need of repair, sluggish and poorly maintained, then it can hamper and distract us from that unity and the joy and freedom that brings. Whatever vehicle we've been endowed with, we need to love and cherish and get the most out of it. "Do you not know your body is a temple of the Holy Spirit" says St Paul,[28] however, it seems to me that we often take more care of our Church buildings than we do of our own bodies, and church buildings are far less important temples than the fleshy ones in which we dwell.

The postures and breath practices (asana and pranayama) of yoga have huge amounts to offer us in this regard, as is increasingly understood by medical institutions and authorities. All the hundreds of postures and varieties of breath work included in Yoga can have positive impacts on almost every aspect of our bodily health and life and are seen as essential for this external aspect of saucha.

The inner aspect of saucha has to do with our mind, emotions and spirit. The cleansing of unhelpful and disruptive thoughts (which can often lead to associated actions), brings healing and peace not only for ourselves but for those around us. For example, within the Christian tradition, the removal from our lives of sloth, lust, anger, pride, envy, greed and gluttony (the "seven deadly sins" first enumerated by Pope Gregory I in the sixth century) cleanses our internal life such that we better reflect that image of God that the Bible says we truly are.

Such cleansing makes us happier, more contented, peaceful and healthier humans.

Unfortunately, the Christian tradition often seems to be resigned to these as "original" sins (i.e. intrinsic to human nature) whereby we can only ask for forgiveness and "with God's help" do better.

This can feel very disempowering to many, and some would say it can create an unhealthy co-dependent relationship with God which can lead to feelings of worthlessness, frustration and depression.

Yoga insists we look much more deeply into sin and suffering to discover its root causes and then do something about it. Its "scientific" (analytical) approach is not so interested in forgiveness after the event, but rather what causes the suffering in the first place. Here, yoga suggests we look more deeply into the workings of the mind and how the body reflects what's going on there. By understanding the root cause, yoga suggests we can work to heal the source of "sin", in other words, we play an active part in our own healing – including the ability to eventually forgive ourselves and others. It seems to me that Jesus's command to "love your neighbour as yourself" is predicated on us understanding ourselves in the first place.

"This internal cleansing," writes B.K.S. Iyengar, "gives radiance and joy. It brings benevolence and banishes mental pain, dejection, sorrow and despair."[29]

Purity, cleanliness, honesty, integrity, health, respect and vitality are all part of saucha, along with the peace and healing that it brings.

Important note: We must not get confused regarding saucha – it's not a puritanical idea connected to moralistic attitudes towards ourselves or others. It's simply about creating a healthy enough body/mind to allow us, as Jesus puts it, "to have life abundantly". Remember, all yoga practice is subject to the first principle, that of ahimsa – non-violence. Any pursuit of saucha that causes violence to body or mind has departed from yoga and become something else.

Invitation

Sit quietly and make contact with your body, that is, listen to it, feel it.

See if it's holding tension anywhere, or pain or aching – often we notice this in the neck and shoulders, the jaw (often clenched), forehead, the eyes, the spine – often lower back (lumbar).

Also, include your inner organs in this enquiry – lungs, heart, kidneys, stomach and so on.

A practice

Sit or lie comfortably and do a body scan by focussing your attention on (say) your toes (each one) and move up your outer body one part at a time (e.g., foot, ankle, calf, shin, knee and so on) until you reach the crown of your head.

If a body part tells you it's in discomfort, pause and listen to it, and promise to return and help.

Having made enquiry into your outer body, once you've reached the crown of the head do an internal body scan, making enquiry of your inner organs – lungs, heart, kidneys, stomach and so on.

That might sound odd or difficult to do, but kidneys can ache, stomachs can feel hot, lungs can wheeze.

It may help to look at a chart to discover where in the body your organs are placed – which can be both fun and educational!

Once the outer and inner body have been scanned and listened to, return to any places that "spoke" to you during the exercise, and offer them some comfort. If stiff or tense, try to relax them/let them go soft, if hot or inflamed, cool them (either physically with a cold flannel, ice pack or cold shower/bath) or imagine directing something cool inwardly toward them (cool air/cool water etc.).

Directing the breath to soften and cool areas is an ancient yoga technique which we'll return to in the chapter on pranayama.

Continue to lie or sit for another few minutes and see if you can feel love, tenderness and respect for your body.

Finally, thank it for all it does for you!

This whole process might take 20–30 minutes (or longer if you begin to enjoy it) – but don't rush through it.

Women are often much better at this kind of exercise than men because every month for most of their lives, women need to listen to their internal bodies, but everyone has the ability to check-in and see how things are.

Sadly, many people have given up any idea of being in contact with their own bodies and instead leave it to medical experts to decipher and treat, even though doctors still need us to tell them something about our pain.

Many people seem to be at war with their own bodies, accusing them of letting them down, not working "properly", or not looking the way they'd prefer.

Otherwise, they mostly ignore them and the noisy voice of the mind overwhelms the body's voice until it's too late and the pain or discomfort finally gets noticed (the body is screaming at this point).

Just look at how many pharmaceutical products there are in the chemist for "heartburn", indigestion and IBS; you will be amazed.

Yet none of them suggests looking deeply into the kinds of food that can create such unpleasant symptoms, nor do they suggest looking at issues of stress and tension in your life (understood now to be one of the main causes of IBS).

So please take time to get to know, love and appreciate your body (it's a miracle of eons of evolution).

The body is not only our primary temple, it's also the vehicle through which we engage with this short and precious life. Having taken millions of years to evolve into what we have now, it behoves us to treat it with deep respect and affection, irrespective of what our troublesome minds might tell us.

We can do a similar scanning practice with our inner lives too.

We can take a look at our thoughts and actions by sitting still and practising "thought watching".

One way to do this is to prepare in the same way as you do when going to the cinema.

Find a comfortable seat and resolve to quietly and attentively watch the screen in front of you.

The screen in this instance is your mind.

Simply watch and see what arises as a thought, projected onto the "screen" of the mind, and without judgement see if the thought makes you happy or sad, hopeful or despairing, disturbed or peaceful, and so on.

Notice any repetitive thoughts, most people develop habitual ways of thinking or doing, particularly in certain circumstances, which they just repeat over and over again.

All the great spiritual traditions have methods of doing this, with one Christian monastic practice offered by St Ignatius of Loyola more than 400 years ago called the Examen.

This is a prayerful reflection usually carried out in the evening on how we've engaged with the day, and consists of five parts:

1. Become aware of God's abiding presence,
2. Review the day from a position of gratitude,
3. Pay attention to your emotions (how your felt during the day, and feel now),
4. Be attentive to any particular event that seemed important – ask why,
5. Look toward tomorrow with openness.

Saucha then is a complex, subtle, but ultimately healing practice addressing the "cleanliness" of our inner and outer lives. It requires sensitivity and compassion as we see and gently work to remove everything that negatively affects our body, mind and relationships, so that we begin to shine with the radiance inherent in all the children of God.

Samtosha

This is the experience of feeling deeply content with life, just the way it is. I've seen this translated as "modesty", which is also a helpful way to look at it, or perhaps "humility" is another way. Samtosha is the cultivation of acceptance of the reality of our situation, not in a resigned way but in a way that harmonises our sense of self with whatever is happening to that self at any given time.

That's not to say that we stay, for example, in situations that are harmful to us, but that in coming to a peace about our situation we're in a better position to understand how to engage with it.

Samtosha is being content with what we have.

I once had dinner with someone in a very nice restaurant. My colleague, however, wanted something that wasn't on the comprehensive menu, and got quite upset when the waiter explained it wasn't possible to alter things in the way they wanted. I was quite amazed – with all the lovely items offered on the menu, the very nice surroundings and the opportunity to enjoy time together, my colleague was still dissatisfied and caused himself, the waiter and me embarrassment and unnecessary suffering.

We do this all the time, things are never quite right; the weather, the strength of our coffee, the menu, our partner…

Other examples of samtosha can appear quite counter-cultural to modern ideas of what brings us peace.

For example, if we believed the media we can only be truly peaceful if we find the right partner, the right job, the right house, win the lottery or otherwise become very wealthy, or famous, or enjoy spectacular good health and levels of fitness hitherto the preserve of athletes, and so on. We all know that even when we've got a new car or better mobile phone, it won't be long before our thoughts turn toward the next version. There's always an upgrade in the pipeline.

And what if we leave home accidently without the mobile, or go somewhere where there's no signal, or we run out of data?

It's a sad truth that should this happen people's levels of anxiety rise very quickly.

The practice of samtosha would create a dispassionate response. No anxiety, frustration or anger, but rather a clear understanding of the situation such that the best course of action becomes clear and unnecessary suffering is avoided.

It is said that the practitioner of yoga looks upon a piece of gold with the same dispassion as a clod of earth. She trusts in life (has faith, *sraddha,* in Sanskrit) and has no need to seek after, grasp or otherwise chase after external things in order for her inner life to be at peace.

She is as happy with a handful of earth as she is with a handful of gold, as delighted by the rain as she is by the sunshine, and internally peaceful even in the midst of external turmoil.

In the end, samtosha requires a deep level of trust – not in a God "out there" somewhere that may come along and save us from any given situation, but in a Love that is inherent in and inseparable from Life – our life.

In the Christian tradition we celebrate "Immanuel – God with us",[30] which means that whatever is happening in the world of "things or forms" (the outer life), the Greater Life within which all forms exist, can be trusted.

B.K.S. Iyengar writes "there is contentment and tranquillity when the flame of the spirit does not waver in the wind of desire". This is, "not the empty peace of the dead, but the peace of one whose reason is firmly established in God".[31]

Invitation

You may want to link this practice with the Examen mentioned earlier, or during thought watching. When you remember an event that occurred during the day or in the past that causes feelings of irritation or annoyance to arise, see if you can create some space between you and the issue, and review it like you might review a film after you've seen it. See if you can look at it with some dispassion, how important in the totality of your life was the event? How much suffering are you willing to accept and live with because of what happened? If such an event were to occur again, how might you be with it, such that it didn't cause you to suffer or suffer so much? Can you imagine the event occurring again and it not disturbing your peace?

Another way is to practise real time. When a situation arises that causes negative emotions or feelings to arise, practise creating space between the event and yourself, real time. One tried and tested way is simply to take a quiet, slow, inhalation, pause momentarily, then gently breathe out – focussing and relaxing on the exhale. I find exhaling through slightly pursed lips (like blowing out a candle but without the force) is helpful as it slows and cools the breath. Just doing this once, or perhaps twice, creates space for the "spirit" of samtosha to arise, if not an actual immediate contentment.

Finally, of course, as mentioned above, samtosha is dependent on faith, that is, trust in Life. God is on your side (whatever your situation or belief system) simply because you're a child of God (you wouldn't be here if you were not). Life can be trusted (which is not the same thing as the "world"), so even though things may not be going your preferred way, deep underneath the chaos, disappointment and struggles, there is solid ground on which you can rest. To practise resting there, is samtosha.

Tapas

Tapas literally means heat, which includes to blaze, burn, shine, suffer pain or consume by fire. Its use in the niyamas is to do with both cleansing, transformation and discipline, and applies to both the body and the mind. For the body, tapas is about looking after its health, keeping it as fit as possible. In yoga this has much to do with heat transforming our food into energy and nourishment (via the digestive process/metabolism), and also "burning up" what is not helpful. When we practise some types of asana (the postures) these can be used to great effect in creating and sustaining tapas, for example, helping our digestive system to process food more efficiently, and breaking down what we don't need and helping expel it. The warmth of tapas created by postures can also relieve muscle tension and other areas of fatigue, preventing a buildup of unhelpful knots and constrictions in the body. Tapas can also be generated through certain kinds of pranayama (breath work), and in combination with asana practice can be a very effective practice in restoring health to the body.

Tapas is equally applicable to the mind. Our minds can generate heat simply by thinking certain kinds of thought, which can be helpful or unhelpful. Consider the last time you became angry. All anger begins in the mind, generated by thought. The mind can almost feel hot as anger grows, and very soon this heat is transferred to the body and we become physically hot, sometimes even our skin can become flushed with the heat of anger. This is a form of tapas, although not usually helpful and rarely consciously acquired (we don't consider becoming angry before the event!).

The mind can generate tapas in other ways. Consider the spiritual practice of fasting. At some point in the fast we may desire to break it because we've seen someone tucking into a lovely looking meal. The undisciplined mind may start to crave something to eat, but the spirit in us (our more conscious self), may say "no, that's not for me at the moment". See how the mind then becomes hot as we wrestle with the desire – the frustration of not fulfilling what the mind is wanting. This kind of tapas is helpful provided we understand what's going on, it's a spiritual discipline that supports our quest to be the master of our minds and bodies rather than slaves to every passing whim. In yoga, the heat generated through this encounter is understood to be consuming unhelpful and unhealthy passions and desires, clearing the way for peace and contentment.

Indeed B.K.S Iyengar writes "the whole science of character-building may be regarded as the practice of tapas".[32]

Tapas can be extremely powerful and needs to be carefully controlled – it should never be used to harm or do violence either to ourselves or any other creature, however, most people don't recognise its existence which can cause problems. Even great biblical figures like Jeremiah struggled with tapas,[33] although in his case he was trying to do good (proclaim the will of God). The purpose of tapas is always to do good – to create and maintain healthy bodies, minds and relationships, any other use is counter-productive and results in unnecessary suffering. In the Christian tradition fire is always understood to be an agent of good, very often associated with the work of the Holy Spirit, burning up that which is unhelpful, transforming what is un-holy into something sacred, creating light, announcing the work or presence of God.

Tapas is an essential element without which life couldn't exist but can be used for good or ill. The Niyama recognises this and seeks to help us work with it, such that it fulfils its task of bringing health and wellbeing both to body and mind.

Invitation

Become aware of the place of tapas in your life – look out for its signs, both physical and emotional. Anger, frustration, irritability, are all signs that there's too much tapas in your life. However, feeling energetic, inspired and ready to engage with life are all the result of a healthy level of tapas. Also, perhaps read some articles on how the human digestive system works, it's critical to your overall health that the digestive process is healthy and efficient. One modern yoga master once remarked that the human body is simply the memory of everything it has ever eaten. There's a lot of truth in that!

Svadhyaya

The fourth of the niyamas concerns self-reflection. Svadhyaya comes from two Sanskrit terms, *sva* meaning "self or belonging to me", and *dhyaya* meaning "examination" or "enquiry".

This is the practice of making enquiry of ourselves, the work of deeply reflecting on our nature and relationships. As svadhyaya can also mean study, we need to understand how that reflection isn't about a momentary thought regarding our behaviour, but a serious and consistent practice of getting to know ourselves. Only in this way can the wonder, miracle and the truth of who we truly are be discerned.

As we shall find out later in the chapter on meditation, when we discover that, we discover who/what everything else is too.

We might also describe this action as "getting close to ourself", which I rather like as a description, because it invokes a sense of intimacy. Svadhyaya isn't the same as psychoanalysis or other such exercise, it's much more like discovering the Love of your life and wanting to find out all about them. It's the practice of looking deeply into our own nature with honesty and endless compassion, both of which are absolutely necessary if this practice is to be properly exercised.

The truth is we don't really know ourselves very well, and what we think we know mostly comes from what others have told us ("you're good at this, you were never good at that"), or our own hasty decisions ("I'm a glass-half-empty" person).

It's perfectly possible for a renowned expert in a certain field of knowledge to know almost nothing about themselves. But whether you're an expert in something or not, most people live and die and never actually meet themselves, which when you think about it is tragic.

The study of the self, however, cannot be confined to looking into our own thoughts and actions without regard to some kind of reference point, otherwise we'll be in grave danger of "missing the mark", which is the root meaning of the word "sin".

Svadhyaya therefore includes the serious study of holy scriptures, writings, and other sources of wisdom. For the Christian this would be centred on the Bible and the writings of the saints and wise elders of the Christian tradition. For the Yogi, the centre would be Patanjali's Yoga Sutra and the commentaries written by the sages and for the Hindu, the Vedas and Upanishads, and so on. However, in yoga there's no bar from reading other traditions' wisdom and teachings, indeed it is positively encouraged. Remember, yoga is not a religion – it's more akin to a science.

B.K.S. Iyengar writes, "The sacred books of the world are for all to read. They are not meant for the members of one particular faith alone. As bees savour the nectar in various flowers, so the *sadhaka* (spiritual disciple) absorbs things in other faiths which will enable him to appreciate his own faith better."[34]

This open attitude for discerning truth wherever it may be found was also clearly articulated in the second Vatican Council held during the 1960s, particularly within the document titled Nostra Aetate. The document includes this paragraph "Let Christians, while witnessing to their own faith and way of life, acknowledge, preserve and encourage the spiritual and moral truths found among non-Christians, also their social life and culture".[35]

Svadhyaya includes the study of all Truth where it can be found simply because yoga is not in itself a religion and therefore has no territory, as such, to defend. As philology is the study of the science of language, yoga is the science of religion, and if religion is seeking after the Truth (of what it is to be alive and in relationship) then svadhyaya has no issue with anything that may help that truth to be uncovered.

In this way, referencing the great wisdom to be found in all tribes and nations throughout the ages, together with the profound experience of each individual, svadhyaya offers us the most beautiful practice of "coming close to ourselves". As we do this, we also discover that we come close to God.

Svadhyaya is the "narrow way" of which Jesus speaks, the way through the self (*sva*) via the elements of study outlined above (*dhyaya*), that opens out into the vast and glorious spaciousness of God.

Invitation

The Christian contemplative tradition has practices designed to support us in the task of svadhyaya, for example, the Monastic practice of the Examen, or Centring Prayer, or the Maranatha prayer practice of John Main. Yoga has its own practices too, all of which stem from the meditative section – the last three limbs – of dharana, dhyana and samadhi, which we'll look at later.

Look into the Christian practices and see if there are any that appeal to you, including using icons, prayer ropes, the rosary, and so on. There's a great deal of wisdom and practice associated with svadhyaya already within the Christian tradition, but it's fine to look at our brothers and sisters of other traditions too.

Ishvarapranidhana

This niyama is of particular importance because it's found not only in the section on niyamas but also has a sutra dedicated to itself in chapter 1.23 of the Yoga Sutra. In essence it means "devotion to the Lord", or a more literal meaning is to lay down before the Lord (*pra* indicates "forward", *ni* "down", and *dha* means "to place (down in front of).

Ishvara is a name used for God or Lord, often in the context of God as the ultimate teacher, holder of all wisdom, and is placed in the niyamas because the writer of the Yoga Sutra wanted to express the truth that although we might practise purity, contentment, discipline and study (the niyamas) with all our strength, yet in the end we'll struggle to achieve a true and lasting experience of union with the Truth without the grace of God. We can't do this alone, and even if we could we'd be in grave danger of attributing our success to ourselves and so completely undermining everything that yoga seeks to achieve. Ishavarapranidhana also implies great humility on behalf of the practitioner (*pranidhana* – laying oneself down before Ishvara).

This idea is connected to the very important yogic understanding that whatever we do, we do it not for ourselves but for the good of all, and in the case of Ishvarapranidhana, to the glory of God. It means to place all our work at the feet of God and not desire or cling to the fruit of that work for ourselves. This is a concept very well understood by Christians and most powerfully and beautifully articulated in the well-known prayer by St Ignatius of Loyola:

Teach us, good Lord,
to serve you as you deserve,
to give and not to count the cost,
to fight and not to heed the wounds,
to toil and not to seek for rest,
to labour and not to ask for any reward,
save that of knowing that we do your will.

"Whatever you do, whatever you eat, whatever you give away, whatever austerity you perform, do it as an offering to me" could quite easily be a command from God quoted in the Bible, however, it's a command from God in the Bhagavad Gita (100–200 BCE), the most revered of Hindu scriptures. I mention it here because it captures the essence of Ishvarapranidhana, that all our efforts need to be offered for the good of all, in and through the grace of God, to the glory of God alone.

Even Jesus asked that his efforts remain secret, not wanting any glory for himself, "Then Jesus said to him, 'See that you say nothing to anyone; but go, show yourself to the priest, and offer the gift that Moses commanded, as a testimony to them.'"[36]

Invitation

If you have a special place in your home dedicated to your prayer time, go and sit there and offer the prayer of St Ignatius replacing the plural pronoun "us/we" with the personal pronoun "me/I". Say it slowly and quietly. Then sit with it for a while.

Take time during the day to dedicate the merits of any action, mundane or not, for the love and glory of God. This could be something as simple as cleaning the house, recycling the rubbish, making a cup of tea or even watching TV (it's a miracle in front of your eyes!).

Begin to make a habit of doing this and see how dedicating an action to God changes your relationship with the object or the action itself. How does such a laying down of oneself make you feel?

For the practising yogi there's a lightness of spirit, a joy and freedom in being released from the tether of self-satisfaction or its opposite, self-criticism.

If you haven't created a personal prayer space, perhaps try making one. You don't need much space – a small table, a windowsill or just the corner of a table will do. Place an object that speaks of the Divine on the table, a small candle/light of some kind, and incense/scented oil burner. Finally put something on the table that needs your attention – say cut flowers, or a little dish of water (which will evaporate after a couple of days). Have a sacred text to hand if you'd like, but nothing more. Use this space to practise Ishvarapranidhana, the offering of yourself and all you do to the glory of God and for the good of all.

Ishvarapranidhana completes the niyamas and so the first two limbs of Patanjali's Hatha Yoga. It's worth re-stating at this point that these codes are not simply interesting additions to the main practice of asana but are absolutely essential to the entire practice of yoga. All the subsequent limbs of working with our bodies, breath, senses and mind, are there to support the practice of the Yamas and the niyamas. This is quite a surprise to the vast majority of Western yoga practitioners, and certainly to those who only know yoga as physical exercise, but if we're to fully engage with this ancient tradition and imbibe its inherent wisdom, we must understand that the Yamas and the niyamas are at the very heart of all true yoga practice.

Without them, yoga is reduced to a personal health benefit or an interesting Eastern philosophy – neither of which represent its truest form or greatest gift. When Christians lose track of what their faith is actually about, and instead get lost in its myriad forms, worship styles, theologies and so forth, the way to return to its essence is to remember Jesus's summary of what the Jewish faith is about, namely "Love the Lord your God with all your heart, soul, strength and mind, and love your neighbour as yourself". The Judeo-Christian tradition has its ten commandments, brilliantly summarised by Jesus in Matthew's gospel,[37] without which the tradition is in danger of becoming an empty vessel. As it is with Christian faith, so it is with the Yamas and niyamas of yoga.

Chapter 5

Limb 3 Asana: (Posture Isn't Just "Down-Face Dog"!)

It may surprise you to know that of the 195 sutras (verses) of Patanjali's Yoga Sutra, only three are dedicated to asana (YS 2.46, 47, 49). Less than one per cent of the Yoga Sutra is specifically focussed on posture.

Again, this comes as quite a shock to those who have only ever considered yoga as physical exercise, but in discovering postures as just the tip of the yoga iceberg, my hope is that as you read through this book and discover more about yoga, you will realise what an immense, wonder-full and wisdom-filled practice this is.

That said, the limited amount of text concerning postures in no way implies that asana is unimportant, indeed like the other limbs of the practice it has its own unique and essential role to play. Without some form of asana there can be no yoga.

Before we have a look at what Patanjali's text says or touch on the immense subject of posture practice as developed in more recent times, it's worth noting that asana (pronounced arsana) doesn't necessarily refer to formal postures taught in yoga classes. An asana can simply be the form the body takes at any time. Sitting in a chair is asana, standing upright, kneeling down, holding your forehead in your hands or folding your hands behind your head, are all postures we take up every day, and these too are asana. The difference between these and the formal postures of yoga practice, are that formal postures are practised consciously, that is, with attentiveness and with a specific purpose in mind, often linking a series of movements and breath together. However, if one stands up from one's chair with complete attentiveness to the movement, with attention to both the idea of standing as it arises in the mind, the body's subsequent movement, and the quality of the breath as we move – we come close to practising a formal yoga posture even if we know nothing about yoga itself.

In the tradition of yoga, postures and breathing techniques were created in order to prepare the body and mind for periods of meditation. We'll look more deeply at meditation as we explore the last three limbs of yoga, but for now it's just worth noting that in order to help quieten (and strengthen) the body and mind, postures and breath control are needed to begin with. As I mentioned earlier in the book, sportswomen and sportsmen use yogic techniques in order to bring their full attention to the task in hand, and if that's the case for kicking an odd-shaped ball over a crossbar, its most certainly needed for exploring our deepest sense of self, other and God. Asana began life not as a way of becoming supple and fit just for its own sake, but in order to prepare for long periods of prayer, which is why almost all of the earliest known asanas were seated postures.

Our minds and bodies are connected; we know that because before we stand up from our chair, we think about it first. First there's a thought, and then there's an action. However, the relationship is much more subtle than that. For example, we also know that when our minds are unhappy, our bodies become unhappy too; dis-ease in the mind often results in disease in the body, as sadly many chronically overweight, underweight, addicted or over-worked people know too well. It's rarely good enough in many such cases to only heal the body; usually the mind needs support as well. Reading through the Twelve Steps created many years ago to support alcoholics recover from their addiction, it's quite clear that the health of the mind is absolutely connected to the health of the body.

However, we don't need to get physically sick to witness this connection. For example, people who feel uneasy in their minds, perhaps through nervousness, excitement or frustration, when sitting down will jiggle their legs. Most of us will have witnessed this in others, and almost certainly done it ourselves.

Others bite their nails, chew their fingers, grind their teeth (sometimes unknowingly when asleep), and so on.

When children's minds are unhappy, they get a tummy ache, when adults' minds are unhappy we often get headaches, sometimes caused by the unconscious tightening of the musculature around the neck, shoulders or jaw. There are many other examples of how the body and mind are interconnected, with scientists and the medical profession continuing to discover ever more subtle connections.

It stands to reason then, that if the mind can affect how the body operates, then the opposite can also be true; that the body can have an effect on the operation of the mind. Again, we already know this because when we desire to go to sleep and hopefully rest the mind (although the two don't always go hand in hand) we need to quieten the body. In sport, when a golfer needs to focus all their attention on a shot, they stand perfectly still behind the ball and only move those parts of the body absolutely essential for the completion of the action. In other words, our minds will follow our bodies if we pay enough attention to the connection between the two. Many people enjoy running these days and it's often the case that runners find a sense of peace when they run. Now you may think this odd, that such an active occupation can calm the mind, but the very rhythm and repetition of the movement, along with perhaps a focus on technique, will quieten the mind. Rather than being fragmented with many different thoughts or feeling dark or heavy with sadness or worries, the mind delights to find itself following the body's lead – focussing on the task in hand and lulled into a peaceful state by the rhythm of the body and the pattern of the breath.

Notice the posture people adopt when they're trying to listen attentively to someone else. Often they will sit upright, perhaps leaning slightly forward toward the speaker, face turned toward them. This posture tells the mind that what is being listened to is important, and the mind obliges by quietening down and ceasing its own internal ramblings (more on this later, in the section on meditation).

The opposite is also true of course; if we're not interested in listening, we will adopt a posture that reflects this, so we might be slouched, leaning slightly backward with our faces or gaze turned away. This tells the mind we're not really interested, and the mind obliges by finding all sorts of thoughts to play with.

There are many other examples of how the body can either support the mind or allow it to drift wherever it chooses, but the key point is that the body-mind connection is two-way, they affect each other and what yoga seeks to do is make that two-way connection a conscious one for the benefit of both.

Asana then is a wonderful way not only to keep the body supple and fit, but even more importantly (in terms of yoga) it helps to train the mind.

T.K.V. Desikachar writes on this connection, "the more we progress [in yoga], the more we become aware of the holistic nature of our being, realising that we are made of body, breath, mind and more. Many people who start studying yoga by practising asanas continue to learn more poses until the only meaning of yoga for them lies in physical exercise. We can liken this to a man who strengthens only one arm and lets the other become weak. Similarly, there are people who intellectualise the idea of yoga ... but they cannot sit erect for even a few minutes.... But if we are to be complete human beings we must incorporate all aspects of ourselves, and do so step by step."[38]

This step-by-step approach includes the practice of using asana to quieten the mind, to help it create and maintain focus, and in the other direction, it helps the mind be attentive to the body, perhaps noticing its "voice" for the first time in many years.

Fundamentals of Asana

The root of the word asana means "to sit", "to stay" or "to be" and evokes the idea of stability or being firmly established in one place. Patanjali offers two basic and essential qualities for all asana, that of *sthira* and *sukha* (briefly mentioned earlier). Sthira is the quality of steadiness and stability, sukha being happiness, ease or joy.

Within the tradition of yoga both these qualities must be present in every posture if its benefit is to be fully realised.

Practically, it works something like this. Firstly, we adopt a particular posture that helps our bodies feel stable and steady – a structure that we can depend on. We then discover the ability to be at ease within it, discovering certain areas or parts of the body, that because they're stable, can relax. Therefore, within the stability of the form the possibility of freedom arises, and within the steady structure an opportunity to flow or even to expand, arises. To experience yoga asana in this sense is not only to begin to understand our own bodies and minds but to begin to engage with how all things are, all phenomena – because it's the way the universe is designed.

Take trees, for example, they are exemplars of sthira sukha. Strong, stable and apparently rigid forms, trees reach into the heavens, and when the winds blow or heavy snow falls, they bend and bow and realise their sukha – an ease contained within their solid structures. Without sthira sukha, trees wouldn't be upright for very long. Human engineers understand this too, which is why all bridges and high-rise buildings also have sthira sukha built into them (I guess there's some technical term they use for this, but Sanskrit was there first!).

In the animal kingdom, sthira and sukha are one reason why snakes are so revered in the Yogic tradition. Of all animals on Earth, the snake's amazing strength combined with its ability to be at ease in just about any position, makes it unique among animals. Indeed, in Hindu mythology the great snake, Ananta, is given the responsibility and joy of carrying the world on his head while making a comfortable seat in his coils in which God can rest – that's quite a feat! His sthira enables him to hold the world with great strength and stability, while his sukha enables him to create a place of comfort and ease in which the Creator can rest.

A note here for some Christians reading this book. I feel it's a great pity, if not a tragedy, that the snake has such a terrible reputation in Christian literature. The story in Genesis chapter 3, along with the ancient Hebrews' fear of snakes, has blighted this wonderful creature for far too long. Do please take another look at the snake – Christians are actually called to be like them! – see St Matthew's gospel.[39]

The more we look around the more we discover sthira sukha everywhere, it seems that every form has its own qualities of stability and ease. We even discover this in art forms and indeed the practice of art, be it painting, sculpture, or music. For example, music has its own sthira – we might call it the musical scale. No one can play an instrument well until they have learned how scales work and how to apply them. But once the stability of the scale is mastered – sukha arises, and the geniuses of music are those who have mastered the scales and then subsequently discovered within that structure the most wonderful musicality, a free-flow of sound, a sukha that could never have been discovered if sthira had not been in place. The same can equally be said of dance.

Another area of life where we discover the wisdom of asana and its qualities of sthira sukha, is that of relationships. Relationships with too much of either, rarely work well. If we're too rigid in our relationship we may hurt our friend or partner by not truly hearing them or properly understanding their position. Or we may demand too much of them and be constantly unhappy because they don't comply with the way we want things to be. On the other hand, if the relationship has no stability, it may appear we don't care, aren't committed to, or are disinterested in their concerns. In order for a healthy relationship to flourish, we need to skilfully practise sthira sukha, creating a relationship on which both can depend and trust and within which both find freedom to be at ease with one another and themselves.

We can also discover sthira and sukha within religion. We've all seen and perhaps encountered religion that has either too much sthira and not enough sukha, or the other way around. These religions are, on the whole, not pleasant or helpful to humanity being either too rigid or too loose, too demanding or not supportive enough. Rather than relieve suffering and moving people toward a greater truth, they actually increase suffering and often keep people stuck on negative and destructive paths. All fundamentalist forms of religion and cults are heavily reliant on sthira without the offer of sukha, which is why, in the end, they break – but not until they've caused huge amounts of suffering. Other forms of spiritual practice that have little in the way of sthira, a sort of laissez-faire approach, are often discovered to be very unsatisfying and people flit from one to another looking for a form of sthira – something to depend on.

In the Christian tradition we discover sthira and sukha in a variety of ways, including within the Bible, Church, and Tradition. Indeed, the old adage was that for Christianity to maintain a healthy balance it needed to constantly refer to Scripture, Reason and Tradition. This was the "three-chord" structure that the architect of Anglicanism, Richard Hooker (1554–1600), offered during the difficult days of the Reformation. If we look carefully, we can see sthira and sukha at work, that Reason must inform Scripture, Scripture must inform Tradition, and Tradition must grow out of both Reason and Scripture. We need the stability of the Bible, but without the sukha of Reason it can easily become a tyrant, and the same can be said for Tradition. In recent years a fourth strand has been added, that of Experience – what is our experience of God, and how does that inform our biblical reading, our experience of Church and its traditions, and our perception of what seems reasonable? Without sthira and sukha, we can find ourselves in a lot of trouble.

We discover therefore that the practice of asana is not simply a matter of stretching limbs and enabling a healthy body, but that its insights and wisdom can inform us about a great many other "postures" or forms that we encounter in life. Asana is essential for linking body, mind and breath, but it enables the fundamental qualities of stability and ease – sthira sukha – to be recognised within the totality of our lives and that of the wider world. Using the wisdom of asana we can discover more about the current state of our relationships across the whole of our life, not just our bodies. Whatever the state of our bodies, breath and mind, the practice of yoga asana can help us to hear our body's "voice" perhaps for the first time in many years. Finally, asana can help quieten our noisy and distracted minds and bring some focus and peace if we're feeling anxious or stressed, or because we're preparing for a time of prayer and meditation.

Asana in yoga practice

Listening to the body

When was the last time you listened to your body? I guess when it was shouting above all the other noise in your mind – perhaps when you were ill and your throat was telling you it was sore, or you'd eaten too much of the wrong thing, or you'd had an accident of some kind.

It seems that for the most part we've forgotten how to make enquiry of, or listen to, the voice of our bodies.

Unfortunately, this brings all kinds of problems because due to the cumulative effects of our "body deafness" we store up all kinds of trouble that might otherwise have been avoided.

Issues with our digestion is just one such area. The global digestive health market was worth 37.9 billion dollars in 2019 and is set to increase by billions more. This area of the multi-billion-dollar pharmaceutical industry is powered (and funded) essentially by human ignorance concerning how our bodies use food, what kinds of food are good for us, and what causes problems for the body.

Just because it seems to taste good, doesn't mean it *is* good!

If we understood just a little about how food works with the body and learn how to listen to what our body tells us regarding what we're putting into it, we could avoid huge amounts of suffering, not to mention saving ourselves a lot of money in highly processed foods and pharmaceutical products.

Likewise, we often injure ourselves because we're not listening to what our bodies are telling us. A knee, ankle or wrist will tell us if it's struggling but waiting for severe pain and then using pills and strapping is not a wise approach and can create permanent damage that may not become obvious until too late.

Another very important area is breath. We shall look at this in much more detail in the chapter on pranayama, however, asana and pranayama go beautifully together. The *Viniyoga* (see T.K.V. Desikachar) tradition in which I was schooled, taught that every posture is accompanied by a conscious breath, either an inhale or an exhale. The body isn't moved into or out of a posture unless accompanied by an in-breath or out-breath, or in more advanced postures perhaps a breath-hold of some kind.

"Bookending" all postures in this way helps us work with our breath such that we become conscious of how the posture affects the breath, and vice versa. As the health of the body and the health of the breath are intimately connected, a practice that brings the two together is of very great value to us. Listening to our breath as we move into, out of, or perhaps hold a posture for a while, can give us great insight into the state our health.

A simple practice: arm raise from *samasthiti* (steady and even pose) into *tadasana* (mountain pose)

Something as simple as a conscious arm raise can provide the opportunity to listen to the body. This can be done sitting if it isn't possible to stand, as follows:

To begin – stand still, tall and straight with arms by your sides, feet hip-width apart and parallel (like on skis). This is a posture known as *samasthiti* (the steady and even pose). If sitting, sit up straight without leaning on the back of the chair and place the hands palms down on the thighs.

1. Become conscious of your breath, simply observe it flowing in and out of our body.
2. Now count how long it takes for you to breathe in (inhale). Just quietly count in your mind how many seconds it takes – could be 3, 4, 5 or maybe 6 seconds – between starting and completing an inhale.
   Do this three or four times.
3. Now do the same with your out-breath (exhale).
4. You may find this takes a second or two longer – it's usually the case that the exhale takes a little longer than the inhale. Again, do this three or four times so that you get a good idea of the time it takes.
5. Now ensure your feet are about hip-width apart, just to give you a firm base. If they're not, just notice how you're standing – is this the way you usually stand? Are you nicely balanced with your weight evenly distributed down each leg, or are you a little off balance, maybe you can feel more weight on one leg/foot than the other? It's just worth noticing this for now, it may be that if you usually stand in a way that doesn't distribute weight evenly it could be creating tensions and perhaps even pain in your hips, back, shoulders or even neck.

6. Make sure your feet are directly in line with (under) your hips, and parallel to each other (as if on skis). Neither foot should be in front of the other.
7. Bring your attention to your fingers and arms, gently pointing your fingers toward the ground so that the mind has engaged the arms.
8. As you begin your next inhale, raise your right arm in front of you, keeping it long, until it's above your shoulder i.e. vertical, or as near as you can manage without any pain. Take all of your in-breath count to move the arm i.e. the 3, 4, 5 or 6 seconds you counted earlier. Your inhale should naturally cease just after the arm reaches its final position.
9. Notice how smoothly or not the arm moved, where it got stuck a little, or how vertical it actually is.
10. On the next exhale, take all of the count (part 3 above) to lower the arm – again pay close attention to arm movement and breath, with the exhale finishing just after the arm completes its movement and is by your side again.
11. Now do exactly the same with the left arm, repeating steps 8,9 &10.
12. Is the travel of the left arm any different to that of the right? Is one of your shoulders a little free-er than the other? How easily are you able to coordinate the movement with the breath – are you finding your breath has "run-out" before your arm has stopped moving?
13. Now do the same with both arms being raised and lowered at the same time, taking all of an inhale to move them in front of you into a vertical position over your head, and all of the exhale to move them back again. Do this four times.

If you've never done yoga before, congratulations on achieving your first two postures! You can now tell folk you know how to do samasthiti and tadasana!

This very simple exercise has helped you to listen to your body and your breath. You became attentive to how you stand, to how your fingers and arms feel when slightly tensioned, how long your normal inhale and exhale takes, how smoothly or not your arm moves, and the shoulders' capacity for raising the arm either vertically or perhaps less than vertical, and whether one side of your body moves differently to the other. You were also able to notice how well you can coordinate movement with breath.

In such a simple way you have begun to quieten the noisy mind that usually drowns out the body's voice so that you can hear its own quiet voice simply letting you know how it is today. In essence this exercise, and indeed all asana practised in such a conscious way, is a profound practice of re-integrating our body, breath and mind such that we experience them as we should, that is, as a whole.

If all of this can be achieved in such a simple posture as an arm movement beginning with samasthiti and moving into tadasana, think of the possibilities that can come with other more exciting/challenging/fun postures later on!

Other ways of understanding Asana

Asana as poetical expression

For many people asana is really only a way of keeping fit, either doing some stretching in the village hall once a week, or for the more energetic types a session of "hot" yoga down at the gym.

I hope the reader is beginning to see that asana can be so much more than that.

Another way of experiencing asana is that of the poetical expression.[40] Many of the postures are given names that represent nature or mythical creatures, and when embodying these, one might "become" that which the name offers. Standing tall, straight, with raised arms, one might become a mountain (*tadasana*). Changing posture, one might become a cobra (*bhujangasana*), or a warrior (*virabhadrasana*) or his bow (*dhanurasana*). Or there's the possibility of becoming a cat (*chakravakasana*) or a dog (*adho mukha svanasana)* or even a lion (*simhasana*).

The point is that the postures are not only inspired by mountains, warriors and lions, but that in adopting such postures one can creatively embody an expression of the mountain, warrior or lion that lies within us. At various times in our life, we need to invoke or express certain qualities that can help us get through a difficult time or find expression for a joyful time. Yoga asana has a vast library of postures that can help us embody our feelings and desires, and through the poetry of these, find holistic expression that can enable our healing and wholeness. This is the beauty of yoga, that there is no area of our life that it cannot play a part in revealing, integrating and making whole.

Asana as preparation for prayer/meditation

Originally there were very few yoga asanas, as mentioned earlier; only three verses in Patanjali's Yoga Sutra even mention asana, and all of these are directed toward preparation for meditation. In order to prepare the body to sit perfectly still for a long period, it was understood that some preparation was needed beforehand. Watching footballers and other athletes before they compete in an event, one can see how they warm up and prepare their body for what is to come. Likewise, if we're going to sit perfectly still for what might be for us a long period of time (the actual length of time depends on the experience of the practitioner – ten minutes can seem like an eternity for a complete beginner!), then the body needs to be "warmed up" and prepared. The purpose of these preparatory asanas is to create the right internal environment for a time of focussed prayer, the body being warmed up and comfortable such that it doesn't cause distraction. In the Christian tradition (and indeed others) the body is understood to be a temple of the Holy Spirit, but temples need to be made ready for worship and prayer, as any good Church Warden will understand! Spending a little time practising some postures before sitting for meditation will prepare the body and the mind for a period of focussed stillness.

Asana as preparation for devotion

Although similar to meditation or payer, devotion has its own particular quality. The etymology of devotion lies in its Latin origins meaning to consecrate, make holy by vow, to solemnly promise, and later on via Old French, to mean "profound religious emotion". Devotion toward another, including God, is for most people the outworking of love, the giving over of one's life or one's "self", through love for the other.

Prayer or meditation need not have an element of "religious emotion" within it, although the very act is devotional in the original sense. However, there are times when humans feel a strong desire to articulate their love or their longing to be loved, and this can lead us quite naturally to a time of devotion. As before, both our bodies and our minds need some preparation beforehand if we're to fully engage with the object of our devotions, and yoga asana can support that. For example, to stand perfectly still in the presence of God, (whether outside in a natural setting, or perhaps indoors in front of an icon or other such object) is to stand in samasthiti (steady and even pose). This standing perfectly still, the body in balance, comfortable, stable, alert, the breath natural, quiet and even, is asana preparation for devotion. Placing the hands together in prayer (Anjali mudra) and placing them near the chest or touching the forehead first before moving them towards the chest (linking mind and heart) is another way of preparing for a time of devotion. Simply leaving the arms by our side but turning the palms outward/towards the front, is also a lovely but discreet way (particularly if you're outside and suddenly feel the call to devotion – perhaps you experience birdsong/starlight etc.). Christians have been using the Anjali mudra for centuries, and within some Christian traditions the genuflexion is also a form of asana (a form of bow) – a posture carried out in preparation for devotion or worship.

Asana as prayer

As well as being preparation for either devotional prayer or meditation, yoga asanas can themselves be prayer. This is an area that some of the burgeoning Christian yoga organisations have explored with considerable success. Often called "body prayer", organisations such as The Christian Yoga Association in the US, and the book *Yoga Devotion,*[41] teach Christians how to use particular postures to help them embody their devotional experience. Cindy Senarighi and Heidi Green authored the book *Yoga Devotion: Practicing in the Presence,* which offers a variety of postures along with biblical quotes and other texts, all designed to support Christians using asana as prayer. There are other such books too, for example, *Maranatha Yoga* by Christine Pickering.

This is a very natural progression for Christians who have always had some element of using the body for prayer, but drawing on the richness of yoga asana with its many different postures and use of the breath further broadens and deepens the experience.

Sometimes words are not enough, they fall short of being able to express how we feel. Humans are much more than vehicles that carry a brain and voice box around, and so the creative arts have unfolded over millennia, from cave paintings in excess of 36,000 years old to those in Tate Modern in the UK, along with ancient sculptures, musical instruments and dance, all offer eloquent testimony to the human need for self-expression. Using the body as prayer with no need for words, music, or explanation – simply expressing how we feel through the movement of the body, perhaps in harmony with the breath, is sometimes all we can do, and that is enough.

Standing in *samasthiti,* hands held in *anjali* mudra, then hands raised heavenwards into *tadasana* pose, and brought gently back to the heart in Anjali mudra, might be so much more helpful to us than a lot of words.

Here is a little sequence I created while designing Yoga for Christians retreat days at Holland House Retreat Centre. It's called **Body Prayer of Compassion**:

Description of the practice

Standing in *samasthiti,* on an inhale sweep both arms out to the side, completing both the movement and inhale when they're above your head, hands in Anjali (prayer) mudra.

Exhale – lower hands to forehead, still in Anjali mudra (take all the exhale to move this very short distance – i.e. move slowly).

Inhale – leave hands where they are.

Exhale – move hands to heart area, continue to hold the mudra.

Inhale – sweep arms out to either side. This should feel like a stretch from fingertip across to fingertip.

Exhale – Return hands to heart area but place palms flat against chest.

Inhale – Make Anjali mudra and raise hands all the way back to above the head (as in position 2).

Exhale – Return arms to side by lowering them in parallel in front of you (rather than sweeping to the side).

The bhavana

You can create your own ideas about what this practice symbolises for you, however, here's my interpretation:

1. Standing still and alert before God and the world
2. Raising my hands in prayer
3. God's mind and my mind become one
4. Placing the mind in the heart
5. Opening the heart to all suffering Beings everywhere (that's why this is an "inclusive" stretch)
6. Gathering all Beings (miss no one and nothing) bring them into the heart
7. Raising the heart-mind to God, now filled with compassion for suffering Beings everywhere
8. Returning to a posture of openness, stillness, awareness

You can do this little sequence a number of consecutive times if it feels right and good to do so.

Asana for listening to the mind

Body and mind are intimately linked; what is going on in the mind very often finds outward expression through the body, and what's happening in the body very often finds its way into the mind.

What arises in the mind lodges in the body, and what arises in the body lodges in the mind.

This being the case, we might use asana to help us listen to the mind. Earlier on in this chapter we touched on how asana could be used to help us listen more carefully to our bodies such that we gave them space to tell us how they were really feeling. The same can be practised the other way around. When we adopt a posture, it may be able to tell us something of our current state of mind. For example, some of the balancing postures can tell us about how still and content our mind is, or the opposite, how noisy and distracted they are.

It can be quite difficult to adopt and hold a balance posture if our minds are very distracted. Something like *rakshasa* (Tree pose) can be very difficult to maintain with a noisy mind. Even something as apparently simple as tadasana (mountain pose) while raising the arms and *lifting the heels off the ground* (standing on the toes), then maintaining the posture for two or three breaths can be a challenge (we "fall off" our toes and quickly place our heels back on the floor).

When taking up such postures, it's certainly worth making enquiry into the state of our minds, not just the body if we're struggling to maintain the pose – especially if we've done them on other occasions without much trouble.

The body for enjoyment and service

In his book *Light on Yoga,* B.K.S. Iyengar reminds us that "the yogi believes that his body has been given to him by the Lord not for enjoyment alone, but also for the service of his fellow men". This insight most surely applies to Christians too, although it seems to me that our problem has been more with enjoying the body than with using it for service.

Christianity has an unfortunate history regarding ideas of enjoying the body, mostly due to being influenced by early Greek and other ideologies, where "Matter" (which included the body) was seen as inferior (or even evil) compared to "Spirit". This in itself has caused a great deal of suffering over the years, and so here we might find some words of wisdom and an approach to being "embodied" that allows us to enjoy the experience.

Iyengar says that when we practise asanas they're to be enjoyed, even if our mind sometimes complains a bit (our minds often would rather we sit and do nothing, watch TV, or listen to music than move!).

When we begin a yoga asana practice, it's interesting to note whether our mind and body are in tune with one another.

The difficulty most of us have is that we listen to our minds much more than our bodies, indeed as was mentioned earlier, unless the body gets sick we rarely hear its voice (it has to shout through an illness to be heard), which is a pity because we'd save ourselves a lot of suffering if we could hear the body's voice more often.

Our bodies are extraordinary and exquisite forms having taken countless eons of time to create (at least 13.8 billion years anyway). I'm aware of friends and colleagues who have taken considerable amounts of time to build cars, boats, musical instruments or even their own homes – and they deservedly thoroughly enjoy the fruit of that labour. Yet when it comes to our bodies, the fruit of billions of years of creative investment, most of us either ignore them, moan about them, are constantly disappointed by them, and some very sadly even hate them. It seems to me that this is a terrible tragedy. Irrespective of our ideas of what a "perfect body" should look like or be able to do, the human body is a magnificent triumph, a culmination of cosmic supernovae, indescribable power, countless experimentation and the ceaseless unfolding of the universe. The beautiful myth of God creating our bodies from dust and breath offered in the Bible provides us with a truth regarding our nature which is absolutely essential if we're to understand who we are and our place in the universe – but it hardly does justice to the detail. The human body, our body, is something to be honoured, treasured and enjoyed. Yoga asana is one way of helping us to do just that.

Asana for healing

Human bodies are both fragile and extraordinarily resilient, however, life can be tough and they can get injured. To support our bodies, humans have developed a great many skills and practices, along with countless organisations created to train people and deliver appropriate care. I hope it can be seen by now that yoga asana can play an important role in supporting the healing of the human body – either as complementary to an existing practice, or in its own right.

Physiotherapy, for example, is used by millions of people both young and old, to help mend, strengthen or create suppleness in joints, ligaments and muscles. Asana can be used to very great effect to complement a physio practice, or indeed to help the practice develop into something which has a greater effect. Employing the breath's support when stretching, strengthening or loosening joints and muscles can add an important element to the effectiveness of physiotherapy, and asana that builds on that can bring the whole of the body into play.

Once the prescribed treatment is complete, asana practice can continue and be developed such that the benefits aren't lost or put on hold but continue, bringing increased benefit and building resilience.

Indeed, there's an entire branch of yoga practice, with very skilled practitioners, that provides extremely good therapeutic services for everyone, from helping injured sportsmen/women recover from injury, to the elderly who need to work joints and ligaments in order to remain healthy.

In summary, old injuries causing stiffness and pain, new injuries, acute or chronic conditions, all can be supported by the skilled application of yoga asana.

Asana and PTSD

Post traumatic stress disorder is now part of the everyday language of healthcare, describing a vast range of trauma related chronic illness. Originally used to help describe the symptoms of war veterans (what was once termed shell shock), it now covers all those who have experienced catastrophic events that have injured their psychophysical health. These can either be one-off events like severe accidents, or longer-term events such as constant abuse. One of the leading experts in this field, Dr Bessel Van Der Kolk, wrote a best-selling book called *The Body Keeps the Score*. In the book he describes how the human body and mind are deeply interconnected, and that the results of traumatic experience are quite literally stored in both mind and body of the injured. People suffering from PTSD often feel alienated from their own bodies, which is a result of the body-mind defence mechanism. Dr Van Der Kolk writes, "the lives of many trauma survivors come to revolve around bracing against and neutralising many unwanted sensory experiences."[42]

The part yoga has to play in helping people with PTSD is detailed in Chapter 16 of his book, titled "Learning to inhabit your body: yoga", where a case study is offered as evidence along with a photograph of a brain scan showing the difference that a twenty-week yoga practice can make.

Another book that is dedicated to the subject of healing trauma through yoga is *Hope: how yoga heals the scars of trauma*.[43] Written by Helen Cushing, a professional yoga teacher, in the light and experience of her work supporting refugees and war veterans. The book lays out in great detail how yoga can play a crucial part in the healing of trauma and PTSD, both the practice of asana and also meditation and pranayama, which we'll be looking into next. Helen writes, "when the stress response becomes chronic and stuck, as it does with PTSD, all the body's systems are adversely affected ... consequently, people with PTSD can suffer from a range of physical ailments ... including digestive problems, back and joint problems, high blood pressure, headaches and insomnia.

"Practices benefitting the body will also benefit the mind."[44]

I'm quite sure many more such books will be written as humans discover the profound interconnectedness of the human mind and body, and indeed the interconnectedness of these to the rest of the Cosmos. To be healed is to be united, nothing that lies in fragments can ever be said to be healed, for healing is wholeness. The science and practice of yoga is certainly nothing less than the work of bringing about that wholeness.

I hope it can be seen then, that yoga asana is far from just folk doing stretching exercises in village halls or people doing "hot yoga" in gym classes. Asana is a multi-faceted, wide ranging, subtle tool that can be employed in many different ways through skilled teachers. However it's employed, yoga asana is there for human healing and development, helping us to consciously connect our minds and bodies such that we may realise a wholeness and a unity previously not experienced. As the final sutra on yoga asana says "sthira – sukham – asana" (Y.S.2.46), which can mean "the posture is firm and comfortable", however, my favourite translation is "with correct stability in a posture, spaciousness arises".[45] Asana, correctly practised and consciously applied, brings nothing less than the freedom to become the beautiful and complete humans we're created to be.

In a moment we'll move on from this third limb of yoga, body-based asana, to the fourth limb – pranayama, or breath work.

But before we do, let's complete this chapter with an invitation...

Invitation

In the Christian tradition, the human body is referred to in the Bible as "a temple of the Holy Spirit".[46]

We spend a lot of time, skill and energy in the upkeep of temples made from bricks and mortar, but these are all secondary to the temples of our bodies.

Sitting comfortably and still (sthira – sukham – asana), consider what our bodies as temples might actually mean?

What are the implications of this insight?

What might it mean for the life and health of your body, how you treat it, how much attention you pay to it?

Also, the bodies of other living Beings – are they not also temples of the Holy Spirit, or are they empty of such Spirit?

How might understanding the body of the earth as such a temple, change our attitude toward it – what might it say about our response to global warming, increased extinctions, the creation of areas of the planet becoming increasingly hostile to human (or other beings) habitation?

What might yoga asana offer us in support of this scripture (1 Corinthians 6:19–20)?

Do try the little asana practice mentioned above (Prayer of Compassion). Repeat it three times and then sit still for at least three minutes – simply notice how the body or mind feels.

If there's a yoga class near you, perhaps check it out, learn a few postures and bring them home. Adapt them to help with any of the issues raised above or make an appointment with someone who's been trained to offer Individual Teaching and Yoga Therapy (this isn't necessarily something a class teacher can do). They will listen to your requirements and help build a bespoke practice for you.

Chapter 6

Limb 4 Pranayama: (The Art of Breath)

We're introduced to pranayama in the second chapter of Patanjali's Yoga Sutra, when he lists the eight limbs of yoga in verse 29. Frans Moors translates this introduction as "the art of breath, mastery of the life force and energy (pranayama), a cornerstone in the practice of yoga and an outstanding tool of purification".

Firstly, it may be news to you that pranayama is a cornerstone of yoga, as most Westerners think that would be asana. Secondly, that breathing can be an art, and that practice and mastery of this art is an outstanding tool for good health.

For most of us, breathing is something that just goes on in the background of our lives – we never think about it until it gets disrupted. When disruption comes, such as a heavy cold, hay fever, inflammation of nasal passages (e.g. rhinitis), or something more serious (e.g., Covid), we very quickly realise how important breathing is. Most people inhale and exhale (one breath) around 23,000 times every day (14–16 times a minute), and every single one of these is important – so important in fact, that if the next breath didn't arise, that would be the end of us. Nonetheless, other than athletes, singers, and folk who rely on healthy breath for a living, most people never consciously engage with this seriously important aspect of their lives.

Yoga understands the importance of breath, to the point that it's seen as the cornerstone of the practice.

It's perhaps worth noting here that this importance shouldn't come as such a big surprise to Christians. In the Bible the word often translated as Spirit is *ruach*, which is Hebrew for breath, and when translated into Greek (the language of most of the New Testament), Spirit is translated as *pneuma* – again meaning breath or wind.

In his book *God in Creation,*[47] Christian theologian Jurgen Moltman writes "the divine Spirit (ruach) is the creative power and presence of God in his creation. The whole creation is a fabric woven by the Spirit and therefore is a reality to which the Spirit gives form".

Setting aside any mystical reference, in just closely observing breath in the human body we can see that it most certainly is woven and held together by breath. Take away breath and the body falls apart, any area of the body not receiving breath dies, indeed lungs, heart and blood circulation are designed specifically to get breath into every cell of the body.

Long before a foetus becomes a recognisable human, the cluster of cells nestled in the womb receives the mother's breath – if it didn't it wouldn't become, as Moltman says, "a reality".

From the arising of a single human to the arising of the entire Cosmos (see Genesis 1.2), breath, ruach, Spirit is "the creative power" in the universe, without which, no universe would exist.

It's also interesting to note that the words ruach/pneuma bring with them ideas of power; that breath carries power or energy.

In yoga this is made explicit in the term pranayama.

The word pranayama comes in two parts. The first part, *prana,* has a number of interpretations, such as vital energy, life source, life breath, or even just Life. Prana is understood to be the energy that we call Life, the power that en-livens all creatures. Through the eight limbs of yoga, we work with prana to ensure we engage with it effectively, through our body work (asana), breath work (pranayama) and mind work (meditation/contemplation). Even the yama and niyama, our internal and external relationships are governed by prana – it's difficult to have healthy relationships if our life-energy is in poor shape. T.K.V. Desikachar sums up prana as "that which is infinitely everywhere".

The second part, *ayama*, means expansion, length, extension, and describes the action of the practice of pranayama. As well as recognising that vital energy extends infinitely throughout the universe, we can, through linking it with our breath, follow the same life force as it penetrates and infuses our own bodies, we are "woven together" by it. Linking the prana that flows throughout the universe with its presence within our bodies, expands our awareness of the interconnectedness of all things. For Christians this can be a very real experience of the truth expounded in the prologue of St John's gospel, that "all things came into being through him", and that "what has come into being in him was life".[48] Rather than remaining a theological idea, the practice of pranayama can be for the Christian an actual embodied experience of that truth. In itself, that can be transformational.

The practice – making it real

In pranayama we focus our attention on the breath, making a deep connection with it using our mind and the bodily sensation of breathing. Unlike the movement of our bodies in asana, the movement of breath in and throughout the body is a very subtle thing and so a clear mind and a still body is very important.

A simple practice

After finding a comfortable seated position in which our spine is straight/vertical, limbs relaxed, head and neck aligned with the spine, and eyes gently closed, we focus on the breath.

We might first draw our attention to the movement of the body as it interacts with breath. We might notice the raising of the chest from the centre of the collarbone as we inhale, and the rib cage moving gently up and out to accommodate the expansion of the lungs. We might also notice the abdomen gently expanding as the diaphragm moves downward beginning the process of drawing air into the lungs.

As we exhale, we can notice the reverse operation, the abdomen contracts as the diaphragm returns to its rest position and the chest falls as the lungs expel the air and return to their original position, ready for the process to begin again. Noticing the ebb and flow of breath as it moves the body in its quiet, natural rhythm is the very first stage of pranayama – the preliminary work. However, simply staying with this has a very calming effect on the mind, giving it some rest from the many thoughts that continually assault it and allowing it to rest upon the natural rhythm of breathing.

Once the movement of the body and breath has been noticed and spent time with, one can then turn attention to noticing where the breath enters and leaves the body. Again, using the mind and sensations, during the inhale we might notice the passage of air over the top lip and into the entrance to the nostrils. We might notice that the air is cool at this point and feel it travelling along the nostril cavity before it touches the back of the nose. As we exhale, we might notice the air travelling in the opposite direction, that it travels a little more quickly than the inhale, and that the air is warmer as it leaves the body.

Again, simply staying with this has a calming effect on the mind, and, also, on the body as a whole. These preliminary stages of pranayama already influence the operation of one of the largest nerves in the body – the vagus nerve,[49] so helping to activate the body's parasympathetic nervous system used for calming us down and preparing us for rest, among many other things.

Practise sitting quietly in this way, paying loving attention to the breath for perhaps five or ten minutes.

See how you feel afterwards.

In yoga, the breath can be understood as the carrier, vehicle, for prana – life energy. Yoga points toward the need to allow the breath to travel easily throughout the body and in order to remain healthy, we need to contain prana. If there are blockages to this energy flow, then prana is forced out of the body (a kind of haemorrhaging of energy) and we become sick. Again, this can be seen very easily in human experience – we all feel "low" or lacking energy when we're not well, and most sickness is accompanied by afflicted breath in one way or another.

On the other hand, when prana is flowing easily and strongly around the body, we feel strong and healthy.

Keeping our airways open when exercising, for example, is crucial if we're to get the most out of our exertions, and learning to breathe properly is a fundamental aspect of many sportspersons' training regime.

Containing and directing prana via the breath not only applies to keeping our bodies healthy, it also helps keep our minds healthy too. The act of generating thought takes considerable energy, as those suffering from deep sadness or depression will tell you. It's very hard to think positively or clearly when you have low energy levels, which is part of the reason why an appropriate physical practice (see asana), combined with a pranayama practice can be so helpful to people suffering from mental health issues.

T.K.V. Desikachar writes "various sources call prana 'the friend of *purusha*' (consciousness), and see in the flow of prana nothing but the working of the purusha. The more content a person is and the better he or she feels, the more prana is contained inside. The more disturbed a person is, the more prana is dissipated and lost".

The quality and health of both our body and mind is governed by the amount of prana we have within the body-mind system. As mentioned earlier, there's no lack of prana in the universe (it's flowing freely around every part), however, the human capacity for receiving and containing it within the body-mind can be limited. Yoga as a principle is about our relationship with prana, and in particular the practice of pranayama is key to this relationship. The practice of paying attention to and working with our breath can be transformative in terms of energising our body and creating a healthy mind, and it is also a practice that reconnects Christians to the very presence of God within us and indeed all around us.

Adam wasn't Adam until he received God's breath (see Genesis 2.7), and so each inhale is a reconnection with the moment of our own creation, as well as the beginning of all human existence. Isn't that a most wonderful thing!

To sit quietly and pay loving attention to the feelings and sensations of our breath is in itself a profound prayer.

No words needed.

Within yoga there are very many practices for pranayama, however, in this book I'll introduce you to just three.

The first will be a basic pranayama practice that moves us on a little from the one described above, and the second will be the next step and introduces a centuries-old practice that both energises and balances the body-mind. The third practice will introduce movement (postures) to the practice.

1. Basic practice: extending the exhale

Take a seated position as described above, spine straight, limbs relaxed including shoulders, jaw, forehead (just notice any tension in these and relax the muscles), head and neck aligned with the spine, and eyes gently closed, focus on the breath.

As you gently inhale simply count how many seconds a natural inhale takes to complete. This will probably be around 4–6 seconds or so. Do this several times, remember not to do anything with the inhale (don't try to extend it, for example).

Once you have a number and you've settled into your natural rhythm, extend the exhale by half as much again. For example, if 4 seconds was the inhale count, breathe out for 6 seconds. Don't force air from your lungs, just relax and let the exhale extend for just a little while longer. In this way you end up with a cycle of In:4 and Out:6 (a ratio of 4:6).

Practise this for five minutes or so and see how you feel afterwards.

Once this feels natural to you, and if you enjoy it, you might add a very short pause after the exhale.

This pause occurs naturally anyway as the breath transitions from the exhale to an inhale, it's just that it's so brief we usually don't notice it. This little addition is not about holding the breath (which is certainly not to be undertaken as it may have a variety of dangers). It is simply about a momentary pause at the "bottom" of the inhale and should not affect in any way the natural rhythm. However, this natural pause is a very peaceful place, so try it out once you have mastered and felt comfortable with the extension of the exhale.

2. Alternate nostril breathing (*nadi shodhana*)

This is sometimes described as "the jewel in the crown" of pranayama techniques, the technique being deceptively simple, but the spectrum of application and its value is immense.

The technique is actually just the conscious application of what the body does naturally, that is, breathing through the left and right nostril, alternating between the two.

During any 24-hour cycle, the body draws breath through both nostrils, however, one is always more dominant than the other. As the cycle continues the nostrils "swap over". If you stop reading this for a moment and quietly move your attention to your nostrils, you may be able to feel which one is more dominant at the moment, that is, which one seems to have more activity, more breath travelling up and down, than the other.

That's often a surprise to people as most think that both nostrils work in tandem, unless one is blocked due to a head cold, etc.

Nadi Shodhana is a pranayama technique that works with this natural cycle. Its purpose is to help re-balance the body-mind and has a purifying effect (*shodhana* is an instrument of purification). *Nadi* means energy channel. Yoga understands that prana is distributed around the body via 72,000 nadis, energy channels, and so nadi shodhana is the cleansing and rebalancing of these channels, which have obviously beneficial effects given our previous look at the importance of prana.

However, even if you don't apply the idea of nadis, the practice of alternate nostril breathing certainly has a beneficial effect on the vagus nerve and the entire somatic system that is the human body-mind.

The practice

Sit as outlined previously.

Engage with the breath naturally as before, simply becoming attentive to your natural rhythm.

Once settled, inhale through both nostrils then apply pressure to the right-hand nostril (closing it with the thumb) and exhale through the left.

Breathe in through the left nostril, close it with right hand ring finger/little finger combined, and breathe out through the right nostril.

Keeping the left nostril closed, breathe in through the right nostril, close it with the thumb, and breathe out through the left.

The rhythm is to exhale/inhale through the same nostril, then change sides.

This might feel a little clumsy at first but after a short time you'll get the hang of it.

Remember that what we're doing is engaging with the way the body naturally uses the nostrils, and that the rhythm of your breath should hardly change from what it is normally. If you feel short of breath using this technique you're probably not allowing your natural rhythm to happen, so just return to paying attention to your natural cycle. Once you're happy with that, try again and ensure that the technique simply aligns with your natural pattern of breathing.

Obviously if you have a head cold or some other constriction of the nostrils, leave the practice until that's resolved. However, even with a slight permanent constriction of one or other nostril (my right nostril is constricted a little due to a teenage accident), nadi shodhana can still be practised. Indeed, in my experience it has helped the affected nostril to widen a little and breathe more normally.

Try nadi shodhana in the evening, perhaps shortly before retiring to bed. It can have a very calming effect on the body-mind and be excellent preparation for sleep, or indeed before a time of prayer or meditation.

The practice can also be very helpful before engaging with a possibly stressful situation, or before an important decision.

Try the practice over a period of time and see where and when it works best for you.

3. Pranayama and Asana

In the chapter on asana, the practice involved raising the arms on an inhale, taking all of that breath to raise the arms above the head, and then lowering them again while breathing out.

All asana in Viniyoga (the practice I teach/was taught) requires us to maintain this connection, that is, whenever we're moving into or out of a posture we do so within an inhale or exhale. Very occasionally we might move on a "hold", that is on a short pause, nearly always at the end of the exhale.

In this way, all asana is connected with pranayama, which provides the fullest and most profound way of practising.

However, we can develop the connection further by moving into a particular posture and then engaging pranayama more fully. Often we deepen the effect by introducing a *bhavana,* that is, a focus or meditation technique that enables us to have a deeper experience of the combination.

Try this little practice

Sitting or standing as outlined in previous practices (spine straight, relaxed but alert, etc.).

Inhaling, lift the arms in front of you (keeping them as straight as possible) all the way until they reach above your head, or as far as they can comfortably go (take *all* the inhale to reach that point). As you do this, imagine that the breath is being drawn up from the ground beneath and through the soles of your feet, up through the legs, torso, spine, arms and out through the pointed fingers and the crown of the head. If it helps you might imagine the breath to be white light.

Leaving the arms above your head, fingers pointing upward (that is, stay in the tadasana posture) exhale back the way you came, the breath flowing down the raised arms, spine, torso, legs and feet. Imagine this breath anchoring you to Earth, creating a strong and stable platform for the next inhale – which might feel like the take-off of a rocket!

On the following inhale, imagine the breath flowing back up through the body as before, through the upraised arms and out through the fingers and crown of the head and streaming into the space above you, endlessly travelling through and touching the far reaches of the universe.

On the next exhale, lower the arms back to their resting position (keeping them straight), again taking all of the exhale to get there, the arms coming to rest by your sides a moment before the exhale completes.

This is a lovely practice to feel both connected to the earth but also to the vast universe.

Christians can sometimes feel confined to the earth as Genesis's account of the creation of humanity is so "soil" based. That's not a bad thing as the earth is certainly "home" for us and we need to feel a deep love and connection to it. However, the earth is made from stardust (literally) and therefore so is everything made from it, including ourselves. So "home" can extend far beyond Earth. Of course, God is present throughout all the Cosmos, not being bound or contained by any "thing", and so through this simple practice we can connect with God as present throughout the vast spaciousness of the universe.

You can vary the practice too, staying for longer with arms raised, or lying on your back and raising the arms skyward. Doing this latter practice on a warm starry night can be a very moving experience.

Anyway, enjoy playing with combining asana and pranayama, and make up your own "bhavana", it's a very creative way to use yoga to deepen faith through the experience of body-mind-breath.

I leave the last word on pranayama to the founding father of modern Yoga as practised in the West, B.K.S. Iyengar, who writes that [the yogi] "offers up the very breath of his being to the Lord as a sacrifice and receives the breath of life from the Lord as his blessing".[50] This most certainly wouldn't be out of place had it been written by a practising Christian!

This brings us to the end of the chapter on pranayama, however, it's a vast and wonderful topic within yoga and we've only really touched upon its possibilities in these few pages.

Chapter 7

Limb 5: Pratyahara: (Freedom from Impulse)

Pratyahara is the fifth limb of yoga and is concerned with the power of the senses, that is, the five senses that humans use to navigate their way through the world – sight, taste, smell, touch, sound.

Yoga understands these as necessary, however, the wisdom of yoga recognises that rather than being useful tools for us, more often they're our masters, to a degree that causes us all kinds of difficulty.

Yoga recognises the inverted nature of this relationship, and that it leads humans into all kinds of trouble and hurt, and certainly away from the healing unity that yoga seeks to help us realise.

This idea certainly isn't new to Christians for whom "the flesh" has become almost synonymous with sin and so endured centuries of castigation and enforced deprivation of the senses in (usually) vain attempts to pacify them.

This approach is anathema to yoga, remember the first rule of yoga is ahimsa (non-violence), so the idea of beating, crushing or hurting the body in order to subdue the senses is certainly not yogic.

Anyway, the fact is that aggressive subjugation doesn't work – not in the long term and causes more problems than it solves.

Yoga doesn't take the view that the body is essentially a problem, as I hope you've gathered by now, and neither does it see the senses as evil and seek to subdue them by force.

Yoga simply understands their power over the untrained mind and seeks to hand that power back to the yogi.

We've all experienced this power over us many times – from walking past a coffee shop and feeling the pull of the aroma, to buying things we never intended to, the so-called impulse buy.

Of course, buying an impulse-led coffee isn't something to be concerned about, indeed it can be fun, however, most of us are aware that the power of our senses over our rational mind can lead to very many kinds of problems, the worst being the problem of addiction.

The issue is that we often aren't aware of what is happening, or what to do about it when we know.

That's because most people don't recognise that the problem lies with the mind (the senses are nothing other than chemical pathways to the brain, which in turn influence the mind). Even if they did, they have few tools at their disposal to help them.

Input from the senses modulates what's going on in the mind, and those modulations can then alter our actions, that is, what we do next. In fact, the mind can very quickly become completely absorbed in its newfound "toy", to the degree that everything else disappears into the background as it obsesses over its new plaything.

In this state we're lost to the power of the object, that is, we're no longer experiencing ourselves as a unified whole, but as a divided being, separated from our deepest sense of self and the world around us by a desire invoked by the senses.

As we've been learning, yoga is about practising wholeness because that's where healing resides, and an end to suffering. Arguably, Jesus's entire ministry was nothing other than the pursuit of healing, both at the particular *and* the Cosmic level (both are the same thing in the end), and he was constantly involved in putting things "back together" again.

Recognising our enslavement to the power of the senses is the first step to living lives that are whole and with less suffering. We create space to experience our true selves, not simply a personality that wants things.

When Jesus went into the desert for 40 days, the gospel writers (Matthew and Luke) have him feeling hungry and tempted to "turn stones into bread". This long fast of Jesus most certainly brought the power of the senses to the fore, and his discussion with the Devil (that is, the "deceiver") is one that we've all had when feeling overwhelmed by the power of the senses.

One image yoga presents regarding pratyahara is that of a tortoise pulling its legs and head into its shell when feeling threatened.

In a similar way, says yoga, we can retract the senses so they're not "out there", scanning around for the next object to grasp.

How do we actually do this?

Well, if we practise yoga, pratyahara happens naturally as a result. Yoga says that pratyahara is a result of engaging with the Yamas and niyamas wholeheartedly, working with our physical body, breath, and (as we shall see in the next chapter) directly with the mind through meditation.

We don't have to practise pratyahara directly because it arises naturally.

When we practise yoga, we help the mind become desensitised to the input of the senses, and therefore the power that objects have over us. It's not that we're somehow "deadening" the senses to external stimuli, but that we voluntarily withdraw them from their constant search for "the next thing". They get relegated to the side-benches, to use a sporting analogy, to be called upon when appropriate.

As the senses and the mind are intimately connected, and as the senses have no power over us that we don't give them via the mind, our ability to understand and control our own thinking is key to us wresting back control.

The work of asana and pranayama together are crucial to building our ability to take back control, as mind, body and breath come together to reassemble the "whole" person that we truly are and always have been.

Objects, discovered by the senses and transmitted to the mind, no longer have the power to divide us from our true selves. Yoga provides the freedom to make true choices, lifting us out from the fog of unfiltered desires and so the suffering much of those create.

All that said, it's possible to exercise pratyahara so that it builds more "muscle", so to speak.

It's easy enough – the next time you're aware of your senses streaming information to the mind about a particular object and a desire to "grasp" it, simply acknowledge that's the case, "thank" the senses (whichever one, in the case of coffee the nose/sense of smell!) and leave it at that.

Don't "follow your nose", just give thanks and move on.

In this way the tortoise withdraws its limbs, the mind remains at rest, and you experience your true self whose happiness and sense of wholeness doesn't depend on external objects.

To learn, practise and most of all experience this sense of freedom, is a fundamental part of yoga, and indeed all spiritual paths. It can bring nothing but joy and contentment in its wake.

Another wonderful benefit of pratyahara for the Christian is that it can reveal to us the presence of God in our midst.

The Christian priest, mystic and poet George Herbert (1593–1633), provides us with this insight through his poem "Elixir".

The third stanza reads:

A man that looks on glass,
On it may stay his eye;
Or if he pleaseth, through it pass,
And then the heav'n espy.

Herbert is speaking of how we might look at a stained glass window and simply see the picture it presents. There our eye "stays" and sees nothing more. This is the work of the senses, simply picking up on the light, colour and form of the window.

However, Herbert suggests we look "through" the object to what lies beyond – not for more objects (e.g., outside the window) but to a deeper truth, wonder and presence that the object points towards.

When that happens, Herbert says we might "heav'n espy".

Pratyahara helps us see "through" form (the object itself) to what lies beyond, because after the senses have discovered it we can lay them down and allow our "inner sense" to discover the "shining source" (as Zen spirituality would name it).

Herbert's wisdom, however, applies to all objects, all forms everywhere. The senses pick them up (which is their task), but we lay them aside to "look" more deeply into and through the object, to what lies beyond.

To see through the "glass" of any object is to create the possibility of seeing heaven, right here and now.

Pratyahara is the yogic state wherein we control our senses, rather than the other way around, and they return to their proper function of being tools for us to use – to help us see clearly, rather than getting lost in the initial "smokescreen".

Herein lies a path to freedom and a new life of peace and wholeness in the lived experience of God's presence in our everyday lives.

The wonderful thing about yoga is that this is a real, concrete possibility born of a practice that involves the whole of who you are: body, breath, mind, spirit, and not simply an aspiration of the heart or a bending of the mind towards a particular theology.

Practice

The next time you go to the supermarket, become aware of how the shop and products are designed to engage your senses and pull you one way or another. Before entering the shop, take a couple of long slow breaths, giving all your attention to the breath as discussed earlier.

Then enter the shop and see just how colourful it is, supermarkets are extraordinarily colourful places – you'll be amazed at the bright colours and shapes of the products.

Notice that products are in places that catch your eye, or they're easy to touch, or indeed smell.

Notice where the bakery section is, how the products are arranged and if there are any "free samples" to taste (quite often cheeses or a new wine offer!).

Become aware of how your senses pick these up and feed the information to the mind via the brain. Investigate what your mind makes of these (which product is it wanting to grasp!).

Notice how many signals the senses are firing off – again you'll be amazed at how quickly the senses do their work, and how the mind copes with it all.

Finally, see if you can enjoy the visit without buying anything at all – just walk around and be amazed, like visiting an art gallery, for instance. See if you can allow the senses to do their work but you remain in control of the outcome.

Chapter 8

Limbs 6, 7, 8 Dharana – Dhyana – Samadhi: (Concentrate, Meditate, Contemplate – the Practice of "One-ing")

The next chapter concerns the sixth, seventh and eighth limbs of yoga, the process and practice of meditation and contemplation. They offer an insight into how to go about meditation, with each limb following on from the next, that is Dharana, Dhyana and Samadhi follow on sequentially. It's not possible to arrive at samadhi without going through the previous stages first, at least not for the majority of people. There are some natural adepts no doubt, who quite naturally and spontaneously enjoy the experience of samadhi and live lives informed by that experience (which is important as we shall see) – but these are very rare indeed.

Perhaps the most important aspect of any religious practice, no matter what faith tradition, is the practice of prayer. Without prayer everything else we do is quite simply an act of our own will – the preference of our own ego. Only prayer has the ability to overcome egoic tendencies and touch the deepest sense of self, the Christ-Self within the Christian tradition, Purusha in yoga, or Buddha Nature within Zen.

In Yoga the principle is the same, to overcome the *citta-vrtti* of our noisy and distracted minds, and experience the deep, boundless dimension of Reality, Life, or indeed God.

Citta (pronounced chitta) refers to the mind, *vrtti* (pronounced vritti) refers to the perambulations, movement, endless thoughts, "noise" going on inside the mind.

Yoga is essentially the work of quietening the vritti, in order to experience Reality/God, and meditation is the primary vehicle yoga uses to achieve that.

The prayer of meditation is essentially non-discursive, that is, wordless (words create vrtti). Meditation is a movement beyond words because words are very limiting things – they're excellent for capturing and holding an idea, but need to be passed through, in order to move beyond the idea to the reality that lies beneath.

I'm aware that some meditation techniques use words to begin with and there's nothing wrong with that, in fact it's a good practice as we shall see, but nonetheless, the word or words are only used as tools to take us beyond the word itself. Words used in meditation are only gateways through which we pass, so the fewer of them the better. Very often the words themselves are eventually discarded as the movement of contemplative prayer/ meditation leaves them behind. We don't stand around in the doorway but pass through to what lies beyond – the "inner chamber" as Christ called it.

It's also worth noting here that by "word", I don't simply mean letters from an alphabet. A word used for meditation might be an object of any sort, a lighted candle, an icon, painting, religious symbol, or an aspect of nature. These are all "words" and as such can be helpful to us in the beginning of our practice, but as mentioned a moment ago, even these need to be "dropped" at some point.

Regarding the practice of meditation itself, in his book *Christian Meditation,*[51] James Finley writes that "the point is that there is no such thing as Christian meditation, formally and officially designated as such, if by that we mean some specific way to meditate".

If we study how the Christian saints and mystics went about the practice, we find that they use the same process as the saints, sages and mystics of other faith traditions. The "words" they use may be different, the "God" whom they seek to connect to may have different names, characteristics and cultural history. But the process is essentially the same, and it's outlined and explained brilliantly by Patanjali in the Yoga Sutra, specifically in the final three limbs of *dharana, dhyana* and *samadhi*. And so it's to these which we now turn, beginning with dharana.

Limb 6: Dharana

This is the first stage of meditation and an absolute requirement if the following stages are to unfold.

The Sanskrit root of the word is *dhr*, which means "to hold". Practising dharana means to hold a particular object in the mind, to pay it close attention to the exclusion of all other thought. As has been mentioned earlier in the book, we see sports professionals doing this all the time – the pro-golfer standing over the ball has only the ball in mind. If they begin thinking about anything else, even momentarily, the shot will not be their best.

When we practise dharana we decide on the object of our attention and then direct all of our attention towards it. In Christian prayer this could be a word from scripture (say "peace"), or an icon, or other symbol. It could just as easily be a candle or something from nature – a stone, or a flower, for example. Or it could be our breath.

We give the object all of our attention – without thinking about it. This is key to success. If we begin to think about the object – what it means to us, its size, colour, history, and so forth, that's not dharana. We're not trying to encourage thought, but to quieten it. Yoga gives us a clue to this process by describing it as *ekagrata*, literally "one-pointed awareness". We simply give the object all of our attention without "colouring it in", so to speak.

We can liken this to times when we need to listen with complete attention to somebody in distress – perhaps a friend or member of our family. When we listen, we're not thinking about anything, we're simply giving them all our attention and opening ourselves to their presence without overlaying it with our own.

In this way we truly hear their authentic voice.

This is dharana, ekagrata – single-pointed awareness.

Yoga sometimes describes dharana as like a diamond that first gathers scattered rays of sunlight and focussing them within its exquisite internal structure, emits them as pure beams of light.

Likewise, as we practise dharana we give an object our complete thought-less attention, thereby stilling thought and all the restless meanderings of the mind. The mind is completely filled with the object of our attention, the mind goes quiet and we begin to experience "that peace which passes all understanding". In all the universe, at that moment, there is only the object of our attention – nothing else.

This single-pointed attention of an object, uncluttered by thoughts, proceeds to the next state which is called *dhyana*.

Practice

Choose an object to practise dharana, or better still allow the object to choose you (by simply picking up the first thing you see). Find a quiet place, sit in a posture that supports meditation, and place the object in front of you. Take some preparatory breaths (exhale slightly longer than inhale – see pranayama in previous chapters).

Now offer the object all of your attention. Direct all your mind towards the object – notice everything about its form, colour, shape, size, smell etc., but don't think or make judgements about those things. Just notice them. See how long you can offer the object your "undivided attention" before you begin thinking again – either about the object or about something else.

I guarantee it won't be very long – a few seconds perhaps! That's absolutely fine – dharana is much harder than we might assume. This experience helps us to see how scattered and restless our minds are, constantly searching the horizon for the next thing to interest it. No wonder we often feel exhausted, even if we don't feel we've done much. If the activity of our minds could be measured in the same way smartwatches measure our steps, we'd be travelling hundreds, perhaps thousands of kilometres every day!

One reason why dharana is such a sacred action is that it allows the object to speak for itself. That is, rather than the observer (subject) telling the observed (object) what it is (via our thoughts, idea or opinions), the object is given the space to offer its own "voice". Perhaps for the first time ever, the object is invited to tell of itself, to speak of its own deepest nature. We probably all know how frustrating it is when people think they know us, name us, label us, or quickly move on to speaking about themselves. But we do this all the time with objects and beings we come across is our everyday lives. We mentioned earlier in the Yamas how easily we can commit a violence against a slug or an ant, simply because we've labelled them a pest. They've no idea about that, they're just living their lives as the sacred beings they are, having the same "Father" as us. Dharana is the loving action of allowing the object of our attention to speak for itself.

Limb 7: Dhyana

Once the one-pointed connection (ekagrata) is established and strong, with no thoughts arising – when the object of our attention completely fills our mind with its own nature rather than our particular prejudices and opinions – the following state of *dhyana* arises quite naturally.

The state of dhyana is the point at which meditation begins, that is, the object and the subject know only each other's presence. The observer gives itself away completely to the observed, holds nothing back, loses itself in the object of its attention, and in the free flow of this deeply intimate connection receives the same in return. No wonder Christian saints and mystics held this form of prayer in such high regard. They may have used a variety of objects (crucifixes, crosses, icons, a particular written word in scripture, and so on), but they connected with it via the technique of ekagrata, and the door that subsequently opens leads to non-other than the *direct experience* of the presence of God.

The kind of deep intimacy that is realised through dharana/dhyana cannot be found within ideas, concepts or even beliefs, because these are all abstractions. They get in the way.

What the Christian (and indeed people of all faiths) deeply yearn for is an authentic experience of God, one that transcends body and mind but is simply not communicable through words or even "sacramental objects". There has to be absolutely nothing (no thing at all) in-between God and human for such profound intimacy to be experienced. Once it has been experienced, there's no going back! We may still use objects to open the gate, as it were, but we now know they're "not it".

The true freedom this brings is extraordinary because we realise we can experience such profound intimacy without the need to fill our minds with *ideas* about God.

"God does not exist within our ideas about God, but has always been exactly and fully God long before humans came up with their ideas." This is what the thirteenth-century Dominican Monk Meister Eckhart meant when he wrote "I pray God to rid me of God".

Dhyana opens the eternal love letter from God to humanity. We may use a variety of "paper, ink or envelopes" to facilitate the communication from our side, but once the communication is experienced for ourselves, the paraphernalia can be set aside as we experience God's presence directly, in our hearts, minds and bodies – all that we are.

This experience leads us to the final stage of the meditative prayer, that of samadhi.

Limb 8: Samadhi

Once we've opened ourselves entirely to God through the process of dharana – dhyana, the final stage is that of *samadhi*, which is the state of final and complete unity. As T.K.V. Desikachar writes, "in samadhi our personal identity – name, profession, family history, bank account, and so forth – completely disappears. Nothing separates us from the object of our choice."[52]

This is surely the prayerful state which St Paul alludes to when he writes "it is no longer I who live, but it is Christ who lives in me. And the life I now live in the flesh I live by the faith of the Son of God, who loved me and gave himself for me" (Galatians 2:20).

The experience of samadhi can occasionally happen for short periods spontaneously.

Sometimes there are moments when our attention is caught by something that overwhelms us. It could be a sunset, birdsong, a rainbow, a child playing, a piece of music or art, the face of the beloved. In those moments all thought falls away, any measurement of time disappears, feelings and bodily sensations dissolve and we're "in the moment" as is sometimes said. The object and the subject "disappear" for a moment or two, into a state of blissful unity. This happens for just a very short time before something distracts us, the connection is broken, and we return to the subject/object relationship. Most of us have known such moments, but we overlook them and take little notice. Yet these are "tasters" of a state of being that is highly significant, it's just that no one told us so.

When we're truly with the "other", when we give ourselves away to them completely (either spontaneously or more consciously), we're not thinking about ourselves, our own preferences, ideas, concerns. Neither do we sit in any kind of judgement on the other – their "otherness" dissolves away. This does not mean their difference disappears – only their "otherness"; I wonder if you can begin to see the difference?

The space between "self" and "other" vanishes, leaving "just this", which has no boundary, no centre, no shape. There isn't even a relationship, because that requires two. Samadhi is the realisation therefore of pure consciousness. There is only awareness, consciousness, complete peace, contentment, restfulness, love.

Love in this sense is not limited to emotion or feelings as human love tends to be. This love transcends human love, that is, it gathers it up and "fills in the gaps". Unconditional love, the kind of love that many (but sadly not all) Christians understand God to be, is nothing less than the complete giving away of the self for the life of the other. Jesus said, "I am the gate, whoever enters through me will be saved; I have come that they may have life and have it to the full" (John 10:9–10).

This gate is none other than the gate Jesus manifested through his life, ministry, death and resurrection, which is none other than unconditional love (the giving away of the self for the life of the other).

It's the gate Jesus offers when he said "I and the Father are one" (John 10.30) and "that they may be one even as we are one" (John 17.11), and Jesus continues, "that they may all be one; even as you Father are in me and I in you, that they also may be in us" (John 17.21).

These words of Jesus could never have been spoken by him had he not experienced samadhi deeply for himself, and neither could he have offered a ministry which shook the foundations of the known world and which continues to do so when understood in all its fullness and glory.

Jesus's ministry, which was nothing less than his life, was a result of a life lived in samadhi.

Samadhi in fact, is the natural, unbroken and eternal state of everything. It's not something humans can create, nor is it actually "achievable" in the sense that we have to do something for it to arise.

Samadhi *is* all the time; however, in order to notice it, experience it, and to live increasingly within its boundless space – we have to find ways of realising it, that is, making it a true, authentic and real experience for us.

For Christians, following Jesus (which as you know by now isn't just being a church-going believer or an adherent to a particular theology), is certainly a way of realising samadhi. However, Jesus offered his yoga to us (as mentioned at the very beginning of this book and which we've explored a little), so that we might be free from simply nodding our heads to doctrines and dogmas that we never really understood, experienced or fully agreed with.

Jesus and his yoga transcend any particular interpretation offered by others – how can his "good news" possibly be contained in exclusive statements designed to defend or uphold one particular religion over and against others?

That type of "way" is coming to an end, indeed it is over already.

Yoga is the way of discovering and consciously entering the truth of Life itself, and the final three limbs of dharana, dhyana and samadhi complete the work of the previous five limbs. All eight are necessary, all eight need to be practised which is why I've included short and easy to access practices in this book.

However, as time goes by you will notice that the limbs of yoga begin to offer themselves in your everyday life, from remembering the call to non-violence (ahimsa) when the slugs eat your marigolds, acquiring the ability not to compulsively follow a strong pull on your senses (walk past the doughnut stand!), to feeling compassion for a being you previously overlooked or maybe even hated.

To follow Jesus and his yoga is to follow the movement of life itself ("the spirit goes where it will"), and in order to follow closely we need to practise our humanity, our being-ness, with all its joys and sorrows, frustrations and delights, hopes and fears.

Yoga is nothing less than the practice of Life, and as Jesus said he'd come that we might have such life "to the full", let us follow him and his yoga together.

> Take my yoga upon you and learn of me, for I am gentle and humble in heart,
> And you will find rest for your souls,
> For my yoga is easy, and my burden is light.

Conclusion "Atha Yoga" and "Now Yoga"

At the time of writing, I've been an Anglican Priest for 19 years, a Reader (authorised Lay Minister) 10 years before that, and a Christian for 39 years. I'm also a qualified Hatha Yoga Teacher.

That's an odd combination in some people's books, anathema for a few, and a "breath of fresh air" to others.

For me, Christianity and Yoga are not separate areas of my life but combine and work together to inform how I respond to Jesus's call to "follow me", a call I first heard clearly in 1991 – the beginning of my journey to Ordination.

Now I find that the wisdom of yoga and the wisdom of Jesus speak to each other in such beautiful ways that I can't separate them – it would be like trying to separate light from the sun. To see the sun, I need its light; to see the light I need the sun – one illumines the other, back and forth without separation.

This is how it is with Wisdom. All true wisdom (which is sometimes called Perennial Wisdom), works in this way. As does unconditional love.

Such wisdom speaks to and illuminates its brothers and sisters within other traditions, no matter colour or creed, time or culture.

This is what I've found; that the wonderful wisdom of yoga speaks to and illumines the wisdom of Jesus, and indeed much of the Bible, because even after nearly forty years of study I still haven't grasped the subtleties of what I've been reading in that great book.

And so it is that I want to share what I've discovered, so that you too might consider making this journey.

Perhaps you're a Christian that already goes to yoga classes (many thousands do) but have never really linked the two together. Perhaps you go to yoga classes but also have an interest in Christian faith, or God, or spirituality in general that your classes haven't touched upon. Or maybe you don't have a religious faith or a yoga practice but have a yearning to discover what life is really about, an intuition that it can't just be about employment, making money, becoming famous, having children, or finding the perfect partner. We might call this yearning, a *Movement of the Heart Towards Love*, which is one way we might interpret the yoga term *brahmacharya*.

If you recognise that you have this feeling, that's a wonderful thing – so hold onto its traces and follow it.

Don't let go or give up on it – it's much too important for that.

The purpose of this book then, is to offer you one way to confirm your feeling is true and to follow it – which is the same thing as following Jesus, which is to take his yoga and learn of him. The first line of the Yoga Sutra is "atha yoga anushasanam", which can be translated as "and now begins the instruction of yoga".

So let's begin, or as Christians taking the yoga of Jesus and learning of him might say "atha yoga Jesu" – now begins the Yoga of Jesus.

Notes

1. T.K.V. Desikachar, *The Heart of Yoga,* Inner Traditions International, p.5
2. John 10.10
3. Matthew 22.36–40
4. Luke 23.34
5. Luke 15.11–32
6. Romans 8:39
7. Luke 2:46–47
8. Luke 4:32
9. Dame Julian was a fourteenth-century woman who received "showings" (visions) of Jesus that she later wrote down as "Revelations of Divine Love".
10. Stigmata are the appearance of the wounds of Jesus, usually in the hands and feet of the devotee.
11. John 11.38b
12. John 17.22-23a
13. Matthew 5:44
14. Mark 12:29–31
15. Eknath Easwaran, *Bhagavad Gita* 3:10, Nilgiri Press 2007, p.105
16. Matthew 6.33
17. Attributed to St Ignatius of Loyola 1491–1556
18. Mark 1:17–18
19. Mark 1.12
20. Matthew 6.5–6
21. Patanjali is a somewhat mythical figure, difficult to date, but most scholars put his Yoga Sutra at around 250–350 BCE.
22. Luke 6. 27–29
23. John 14.6
24. John 8:32
25. Joseph Fletcher *Situation Ethics* SCM Press, Bloomsbury Street London, p.69

26. Georg Feuerstein *The Deeper Dimension of Yoga*, Shambala Boulder 2003, p.290
27. Galatians 5:23
28. 1 Corinthians 6.19
29. B. K. S. Iyengar, *Light on Yoga*, Harper Collins, 1 London Bridge Street, London, p.16
30. Matthew 1:23
31. B. K. S. Iyengar, *Light on Yoga*, Harper Collins, 1 London Bridge Street, London, p.18
32. Ibid p.18
33. See Jeremiah 20:9
34. Ibid p.19
35. *Vatican Council II*, Pillar Books © Costello Publishing Co 1975. P739
36. Matthew 8.4
37. Matthew 22:34–40
38. T.K.V. Desikachar, *The Heart of Yoga*, Inner Traditions International, p. 7
39. Matthew 10.16
40. My thanks to Dave Charlton and Ranju Roy for this insight. See *Embodying the Yoga Sutra*, YogaWords Pinter & Martin Ltd 2019, p.164
41. Cindy Senarighi and Heidi Green, *YogaDevotion*, Credo House Publishers 2017, Grand Rapids, Michigan
42. Bessel van der Kolk, *The Body Keeps the Score*, Penguin Books 2015, p.265
43. Helen Cushing, *Hope, How Yoga Heals the Scars of Trauma*, Ganges Yoga, Hobart Australia 2016.
44. Ibid, page 52–53.
45. Embodying the Yoga Sutra p. 162
46. 1 Corinthians 6:19
47. Jurgen Moltmann, *God in Creation*, SCM Press 1985, p99
48. John 1.3–4

49. The vagus nerve is the longest of the 12 cranial nerves and represents the main component of the parasympathetic nervous system, which oversees a vast array of crucial bodily functions.
50. B. K. S. Iyengar, *Light on Yoga,* Harper Collins, 1 London Bridge Street, London, p. 23
51. J Finley, *Christian Meditation,* Harper Collins, 10 East 53rd Street, New York, 2004, p. 23
52. T.K.V. Desikachar, *The Heart of Yoga,* Inner Traditions International, p. 109

Bible quotations are from the New Revised Standard Version, Oxford University Press 1995

Further Reading

A Meeting of Mystic Paths: Christianity and Yoga: Justin O'Brien, Penguin, 1989

The Yoga Sutras of Patanjali: Translated and Introduced by Alastair Shearer, Rider (Ebury Press London), 2010.

Reclaiming Spirituality: Diarmuid O'Murchu: The Crossroad Publishing Company, New York, 1998

About the Author

After a short career in the Royal Navy, and a rather longer one in I.T., Ian was accepted, trained and ordained into the Anglican Church in 2005. He remained in full time ministry until 2023 when he retired. After serving his curacy at Great Malvern Priory, he became Priest and Warden of the award-winning Holland House Retreat House in the Diocese of Worcester. As well as managing the business Ian also created and ran retreats on Christian mystics, Yoga, Zen and Contemplative prayer. He's a trained Yoga Teacher authorised by the Association for Yoga studies (AYS) and a long-time student and practitioner of Zen where he's currently undergoing training as a Zen Teacher (Sensei) with the Wild Goose Zen Sangha, part of the international White Plum Asangha Association of Zen Teachers.

Ian continues to offer retreats, quiet days, talks and Spiritual Accompaniment (one to one work) drawing on his Christian Contemplative, Yoga and Zen experience. You can find out more about this ministry by visiting his website at www.the boundlessway.co.uk.

MANTRA
BOOKS

EASTERN RELIGION & PHILOSOPHY

We publish books on Eastern religions and philosophies. Books that aim to inform and explore the various traditions that began in the East and have migrated West.

If you have enjoyed this book, why not tell other readers by posting a review on your preferred book site.

Recent Bestsellers from MANTRA BOOKS Are:

The Way Things Are

A Living Approach to Buddhism

Lama Ole Nydahl

An introduction to the teachings of the Buddha, and how to make use of these teachings in everyday life.

Paperback: 978-1-84694-042-2 ebook: 978-1-78099-845-9

Back to the Truth

5000 Years of Advaita

Dennis Waite

A demystifying guide to Advaita for both those new to, and those familiar with this ancient, non-dualist philosophy from India.

Paperback: 978-1-90504-761-1 ebook: 978-184694-624-0

Shinto: A celebration of Life

Aidan Rankin

Introducing a gentle but powerful spiritual pathway reconnecting humanity with Great Nature and arming all aspects of life.

Paperback: 978-1-84694-438-3 ebook: 978-1-84694-738-4

In the Light of Meditation

Mike George

A comprehensive introduction to the practice of meditation and the spiritual principles behind it. A 10 lesson meditation programme with CD and internet support.

Paperback: 978-1-90381-661-5

The 7 Levels of Wisdom

Mónica Esgueva

A straightforward and compelling approach on how to reach the highest levels of consciousness, wisdom, and inner peace.

Paperback: 978-1-80341-470-6 ebook: 978-1-80341-471-3

Compassion Based Living Course

Heather Regan-Addis and Choden

A practical guide to living a compassionate life.

Paperback: 978-1-80341-676-2 ebook: 978-1-80341-709-7

The Sacred Gathas of Zarathushtra & the Old Avestan Canon

Pablo Vazquez

The ancient and mystical poetry of Zarathushtra and the first Zoroastrians: Now accessible to the public in a modern translation.

Paperback: 978-1-78535-961-3 ebook: 978-1-78535-962-0

Radiant Bliss

Sue Bushell

Embrace Your Journey: Unfolding Peace, Power, and Purpose Through Yoga

Paperback: 978-1-80341-818-6 ebook: 978-1-80341-822-3

Ordinary Women, Extraordinary Wisdom
Rita Marie Robinson
The Feminine Face of Awakening
A collection of intimate conversations with female spiritual teachers who live like ordinary women, but are engaged with their true natures.
Paperback: 978-1-84694-068-2 ebook: 978-1-78099-908-1

The Riddle of Alchemy
Paul Kiritsis
What is alchemy, exactly? Is there any empirical truth to ancient speculative pursuits toward metallic transmutation? How does alchemy intersect with Western mind sciences and science in general?
Paperback: 978-1-80341-637-3 ebook: 978-1-80341-688-5

Readers of ebooks can buy or view any of these bestsellers by clicking on the live link in the title. Most titles are published in paperback and as an ebook. Paperbacks are available in traditional bookshops. Both print and ebook formats are available online.

Find more titles and sign up to our readers' newsletter at www.collectiveinkbooks.com/mind-body-spirit. Follow us on Facebook at facebook.com/OBooks and Twitter at twitter.com/obooks